LIFE AT NUMBER 10

MAINSTREAM *SPORT*

LIFE AT NUMBER 10

AN AUTOBIOGRAPHY

NEIL JENKINS WITH PAUL REES

MAINSTREAM
PUBLISHING

EDINBURGH AND LONDON

First published in Great Britain in 1998 by
MAINSTREAM PUBLISHING COMPANY (EDINBURGH) LTD
7 Albany Street
Edinburgh EH1 3UG

This edition 1999

ISBN 1 84018 245 8

A catalogue record for this book is available from the British Library

Typeset in Sabon
Printed and bound in Finland by WSOY

To my parents, Cath and the memory of my
grandfather, Sid Chinnock

Contents

Acknowledgements

The authors thank the following for their help and support in the preparation of this book: Eileen and Roger Jenkins, Catherine Jenkins, Andrew Chinnock, Peter Chinnock, Ruth Chinnock, Andrew Harry, Jason Williams; Bernard Jones and Gerald Coleman of Just Rentals; Dr Alan Granfield, Eddie Jones, Cenydd Thomas, Dennis John and the staff at Pontypridd RFC; Huw Llewellyn of Adidas; Alan Edmunds, Richard Morgans and Sally Uphill of *Wales on Sunday*; Huw Evans; Ian Malin of *The Guardian*; Cathy Mineards and Bill Campbell at Mainstream Publishing; and Howard Evans, rugby statistician *par excellence*.

Field of Dreams

Your throat is dry, your cheeks are burning, you feel breathless. All that stands between you and glory is an oval-shaped ball and a set of posts. You sense the nervousness of the crowd, some of whom are willing you to succeed while others are doing their best to put you off. You wonder why you are not sitting in front of the television with your feet up, clutching a can of cold beer and watching someone else audition for a part he is not sure of: hero or fall guy.

You only wonder for a second. You blot out the noise, the nerves, the tension and the occasion. You pretend you are somewhere else, long ago, when nobody apart from your family and your school friends had ever heard of you. You are in a park not far from your home practising your goal-kicking. No one is around apart from a couple of souls walking their dogs, but they do not take even a cursory interest. There is nothing at stake: you can miss everything and tell your father you were unerringly accurate. Only you know.

In the summer of 1997 I was at Newlands in Cape Town, King's Park in Durban and Ellis Park in Johannesburg, playing for the British and Irish Lions against South Africa and taking the kicks at goal as we looked to achieve what only one Lions side had managed to achieve before: to snare the Springboks in their own lair. But when the moment of reckoning came, I was not in South Africa but on Cae Fardre, the field near the house where I was brought up in South Wales and where I spent many hundreds of hours alone with a rugby ball.

The irony was that when I was a teenager at Cae Fardre I imagined I was at Cardiff Arms Park, having been given the kick which would beat England, 50,000 souls watching me with bated breath. I never missed, but in South Africa the dream became virtual reality: the venue was different and I never had a kick to win a match, but in Durban I had one attempt to tie the score and keep us in the game.

I was back at Cae Fardre, no noise, no distractions, no pressure. I took a few deep breaths and shook my arms as they hung straight down in front of me, and I could hear the roar of the crowd as the ball went over. I could even hear a strain of 'Bread of Heaven'. And I was in heaven.

CHAPTER ONE

Harold

Bliss it was to be a boy growing up in South Wales during the 1970s. Rugby union had been the Welsh currency for nigh on 100 years and the interest rate was booming. I made my first appearance in July 1971, one of the greatest years in the history of the game in Wales. We had won the Grand Slam for the first time since 1952 and the nucleus of that side was at the time of my birth in East Glamorgan Hospital helping create history by becoming the first Lions team to win a Test series in New Zealand: J.P.R. Williams, John Dawes, Gerald Davies, Barry John, Gareth Edwards, Delme Thomas, Mervyn Davies and John Taylor. They were names, and faces, which became etched on my mind from an early age, together with those of Phil Bennett and J.J. Williams, whose years were to come. Wales was a land of rugby heroes and, though I was not to know it then, a fateful legacy was being sown for international players of the future. Milestones became millstones.

As the relative failure of the 1980s turned into the despondency of the 1990s, players of my generation were constantly reminded of the successes of the 1970s. With a few exceptions, the leading players of that era had carved out careers in the media, and instead of receding in the national consciousness, the memories of that age loomed ever large. The pity was that so few of the players had put anything back into the game directly. They played in an age when rugby union was nominally amateur and their punishment for cashing in on their fame by writing books or newspaper columns was permanent ostracism from the sport. They were

13

deemed professionals whose hands would taint the purity of those playing the game, something which now appears ludicrous given the multi-million-pound business rugby union has become in each of the major nations.

The pity is that the trend is still continuing. Jonathan Davies, the best player produced by Wales in the last 20 years, retired at the end of the 1996–97 season, but his knowledge and acumen have not been exploited by the game. Instead his contribution is made through the media, a costly waste at a time when we have to make the most of our resources if a country which has over the years been the strongest in the Five Nations is not to fall so far behind the top five, New Zealand, South Africa, Australia, France and England, that they are out of sight.

I made my international début in 1991, a year which has probably gone down as the worst in Wales's history, a shambolic period which ended ignominiously that summer in Brisbane when, having been thumped on the pitch by Australia 63–6, a scoreline which would have been 75–6 in today's values, some of our players tried to thump each other during the post-match function. I returned home from that trip in despair. As a young boy pestering his father to take him to rugby matches, playing at being Barry John or Phil Bennett in the streets with anything from a ball to a rolled-up piece of paper, being capped by Wales had been my dream and I remember wondering on the flight home, anticipating the lurid headlines which were going to greet us on our arrival, what we were leaving for the players of the future.

How had it turned around so quickly? It was only in 1978 that Wales had won the Grand Slam in emphatic style against France, a year they would have beaten New Zealand in Cardiff but for blatant cheating by the All Blacks at the end of the 80 minutes which gave them a penalty and an undeserved victory. Here we were, just 13 years later, the laughing stock of the rugby world, a pitiful sight, commanding no respect on the field and with no self-respect off it. I did not expect to remain long in Wales: rugby league beckoned and, at that time, it looked a more than attractive alternative, a game in which you did not receive beatings for nothing.

As a young boy, seduced by the moment, rugby was everything to me. I saw my first game when I was six, begging my father, Roger, to take me to watch my favourite team, Cardiff, until he at last relented. Even though I lived in Llantwit Fadre, near Pontypridd, and went to school in neighbouring Beddau, Cardiff were my team and I wanted nothing more than to pull on a blue and black jersey.

I grew up in a rugby-mad environment: my father had had Welsh Schools trials and tells me that he was a more than useful flanker and that only size prevented him from progressing beyond junior rugby. My mother, Eileen, was also steeped in the game. Her brothers, my uncles Peter and Andrew, two men who have had a profound influence on my career, both played the game to a decent level, Andrew a regular for Pontypridd's reserve side.

When I first saw Cardiff in 1978, they were playing at Pontypool in the Welsh Cup, the best pack in British rugby taking on a slick set of backs. Why I favoured Cardiff I do not know, but their outside half, Gareth Davies, was my favourite player and perhaps, even though my career in Wales was forged at Ponty-pridd, an unfashionable club, I was attracted by glamour. I have always been an avid Manchester United supporter and have followed the Wigan rugby league side for years. Glamour there was at Pontypool Park that day. I remember little about the game itself except that the ground, the most picturesque in Wales with its rolling hills and grassy banks, was full to capacity. The crowd generated a noise which was at first unnerving, especially when spectators took exception to the referee, but the rugby was compelling. Cardiff were taken apart at forward, but they won the tie 16–11. Gerald Davies, the prince of wings, touched the ball four times and scored four tries.

What made an impact on me that day was the contrast between the intensity of the forward battle, big men hammering into each other, contesting set-pieces and breakdowns as if they were at war, and the slight figures behind the scrum, like Gareth Davies and Gerald Davies, who watched the forward scrap as if with bemusement before taking the ball into another dimension on the few occasions they received it. I was fascinated by this game of brutal beauty, Pontypool battering away at Cardiff's line time and again, but all they had for their efforts was the sight of the number 14 on Gerald's jersey as he ran in the tries.

It is eerie to look back and reflect that those players did it all for nothing, save for a few beers and grubby envelopes. They all had jobs, rugby was to them a pastime and yet, for a couple of pounds, a spectator was granted an audience with some of the best players in the world, some of the most gifted performers the game had ever seen. What would a Gerald Davies be worth today? The game at the top may be professional, but the base on which the game in Wales was built in the 1970s has shrunk to such an extent that the means to pay players, which was there a generation ago, is barely sufficient today, with some clubs desperately trying to stave off bankruptcy.

Welsh rugby has contracted: fewer clubs at the top (when Wales won the Triple Crown against Ireland in 1965, 11 clubs were represented in the side; when we played France at the end of the 1998 championship, the side was chosen from just four clubs); fewer spectators, though Pontypridd have been an exception to that trend thanks to what I consider to be the best supporters in Britain; and consequently fewer players of international quality, because they are not playing in a properly competitive environment. I firmly believe that the narrowing of the plinth upon which the Welsh club game is mounted has contributed in no small measure to our marginalisation as an international force. Whereas Welsh rugby had the virtue of self-help up until the end of the 1970s, we now have to look to others to help make us strong: the European Cup and the Anglo-Welsh league. No longer does the answer lie within.

If I have had the misfortune of representing Wales at a time of unprecedented decline, growing up in South Wales in the 1970s was all about making it on to the field of dreams: Cardiff Arms Park. Whereas today kids playing in the streets will be decked out in the kits of leading soccer clubs, when I was a boy rugby was all the rage. I played my first game when I was seven. I joined the Llantwit Fadre mini-rugby team. It was coached by Dennis John, who at the end of 1991 became the coach of Pontypridd, and his son Paul, my half-back partner at club and international level throughout the 1990s, was in the side.

I had wanted to play before, but we were not allowed to in school. I always played in the backs, often on the wing because I was quite quick in those days. My parents were keen for me to play and I was fortunate that the set-up in Llantwit Fadre was a strong one. We would play tournaments in England at clubs such as Moseley and Worcester, our big rivals where the battles were nothing but hard fought. Even at that tender age you were taught that winning mattered, never mind the taking part. Welsh rugby was a serious business. Beddau was our biggest game of the season. Local pride meant you had to take your time returning home if you lost.

I played a bit of soccer and when I was 11 I had to choose between the two codes of football which were played in South Wales: association or rugby. I had been offered a place in the Pontypridd Under-11 soccer team, but I could not play both football and rugby. There was no choice. Manchester United was a distant dream; the Arms Park was on my doorstep. Rugby was real; soccer was little more than a sticker book. You are a product of your heritage – which is why I am so fearful of what lies ahead for Welsh rugby.

Television has ensured that the leading soccer clubs have a meaning to kids beyond playground rivalry. The Premier Division in England is one of the business success stories of the 1990s and on every terrace at a major Welsh club rugby match you will see boys and girls wearing replica soccer jerseys. A sport has to win the hearts and minds of the young if it is to thrive, but all that rugby in Wales has been about in recent years has been failure on the international field and the constant feuding off it between the clubs and the Welsh Rugby Union which has yielded a welter of bad publicity. Sport is about the future as much as the present, but Welsh rugby failed to invest when it was at the top and those running the game then bequeathed to posterity a squandered legacy.

It was well that I showed an aptitude for sport at an early age because I was no academic at school. I regarded education as a form of national service and I was always going to leave the moment my conscription period ended. The teachers at Bryn Celynnog Comprehensive in Beddau tried their best with me. I sat a couple of GCSEs, but the only lessons I enjoyed were PE and, surprisingly, RE. Most of my friends were rugby players and we all ended up in the lower sets, more interested in balls than books, but my best mate was, and still is, Jason Williams.

He had cerebral palsy and so he could not play sport. He went through a gruelling series of operations and he was an inspiration to me because, despite everything, he was always a cheerful lad, full of optimism. I suppose he had to be because he was an avid Cardiff City fan, but Jason made me realise how fortunate I was. Sport dominated both our lives, but only I would have the chance to fulfil my dreams. We are still close and I think it is important that, no matter how successful you are in your particular field, you should never forget your roots. A sadness for me is that even though I still live in close proximity to a number of the friends I grew up with, many of us have grown apart. You cannot stand still, but I still think of the Sundays I spent with Paul Vowles, rattling up and down the M6 to see Wigan, first with his father Tudor acting as chauffeur because we were too young to drive, and then in his battered Fiat. Central Park was like a second home to us.

In my latter days at school, I used to take time off regularly, persuading my mother to write another sick note so I could help my father in his scrap metal business. She would give me a lecture, but she knew by then I was going to get my education in the university of life. I remember one day, when I was at school, returning to class having won an area penalty shoot-out in soccer. I was presented with a big trophy and was feeling pleased with myself when I sat down for an English lesson. The teacher looked at the cup, smiled and said in her best put-down voice, 'What a lovely trophy. A pity this essay of yours is not up to scratch.' I was 14 then, looking forward to the day when I no longer had to go to school. I left without qualifications, but I have no regrets. I grew up working with my father: loading a skip, wielding a sledgehammer, driving a lorry and minding the yard for him when he was out making deliveries.

He had a yard in Church Village, near our home. My grandfather had had a haulage company and it turned into a scrap metal concern. The lorries were parked in a big field and I used to play there regularly when I was young. The pleasure of winning my first cap was tempered by the fact that my father was about to go bust and that I would have to start thinking about a career off the field. We used to deal with the collieries in Cwm and Beddau as well as bus companies. Aluminium brought in big money at that time, but the writing was on the wall for us as the fallout from the 1984 miners' strike settled and pits closed. I used to bunk off school to help my father in the yard or go in the lorry delivering with him to various parts of England. We went to Nottingham, Bedford and Birmingham a lot delivering axles and engines, trundling along the motorways at no more than 60 mph because the loads were so big.

Working for my father meant I was naturally fit to play rugby, even if the sight of me humping loads around in greasy overalls did not conjure up the image of an heir to the Wales outside-half crown. By the time I started working for my father full-time, I was settled in the Pontypridd Youth squad and would turn up to training unshaven and covered in oil. The other players dubbed me Harold after the character in *Steptoe and Son* and I suppose I did look a sight, but they were great days which I look back on fondly: the sight of my Auntie Cennys, who had an HGV licence, driving a lorry to the Midlands; my grandfather sitting me down after a hard day's work with a sandwich which looked as if it had been made from a whole loaf of bread; the stories told in the Farmer's Arms and the laughter; the gypsies who used to try to take advantage of a raw teenager when I was looking after the yard in my father's absence; and the freedom of fresh air away from the stuffy classroom. I was where I belonged but it was not to last. I do not like to think what would have happened had I not made it as a rugby player because I had nothing to fall back on.

The day I regained my place in the Wales team, at the beginning of 1992, had seen me start work as a tiler. Pontypridd had got me the job and my boss was Roger Jennings. He used to do up old council houses and it was hard, after working for my father and the freedom that brought, to have a stranger as a gaffer. I was sticking up tiles on my first day, listening to the radio.

The sports news came on and they announced the team to play Ireland the following week. The announcer said that several changes had been made following the unsuccessful World Cup campaign and that Llanelli's Colin Stephens would be the outside half. I thought that was that and went back to the tiling, but when he read out the team and I heard I was in the centre, I was jumping all over the place. I went up to Roger and told him I was going home to prepare for the game and he looked at me and said I could not finish. I said he had seen the last of me and cheekily asked him if he could drop me off at home so I could practise my goal-kicking. A night on the tiles was one thing, but not a day on them!

The next time I worked was for Just Rentals, another job secured for me by Pontypridd, and it was the understanding and consideration of the company's management which helped me put in the effort I needed to become a successful rugby player. Some are born to reach the top but I had to work hard to get there.

CHAPTER TWO

Black but Not Blue

M y dream of playing for Cardiff died when I was 15 only to be resurrected 13 years later. Until then, I had followed the club regularly. They were the dominant force in the Schweppes Cup from 1981 and most years I would enjoy a day out for the final at the National Stadium, which they invariably won. Welsh rugby may not have had leagues in those days, but it had a buzz. Cardiff and Pontypool were the two strongest teams in Wales and, in 1985, they met for an effective title decider at the Arms Park. Cardiff had built themselves a pack which was more than capable of looking after itself and they still had a rapier thrust behind, while Pontypool were what they always had been: strong, confrontational and single-minded.

The match was played on a Wednesday night, a tradition which has virtually ended in Wales now, which again makes you marvel at how players managed it in the days of amateurism: two matches a week, training and a job to hold down, not to mention the responsibilities of family life. The build-up to the match was intense and there was no way I was going to miss out. The contest within a contest was at scrum half, where Terry Holmes, the Wales captain who was soon to turn professional with Bradford Northern, was coming up against one of the pretenders to his throne, David Bishop, the *enfant terrible* of Welsh rugby, a player of such athleticism and strength that he would have won many more caps than the solitary one he gained in 1984 had it not been for various indiscretions on and off the field.

So many spectators wanted to see the match that huge queues

built up outside the turnstiles long before the kick-off. Two things became clear as the start neared: not everyone was going to get in, and some of those who were would not see the beginning of the match – but there was no way anyone was going to miss the action. The crowd stormed the gates, clambering over fences and across the top of the turnstile booths. The capacity of the ground was 14,500 but they reckoned some 20,000 saw the showdown, which was as raw, full-blooded and close as had been expected. Holmes failed to last the course. He ran down the wing and ahead of him stood Chris Huish, a flanker who made the Incredible Hulk look like a model in a Ryvita advert. Holmes was all sinew and muscle – the unstoppable against the immovable – and I can still hear the collision now. Neither player gave an inch but Holmes's shoulder gave out.

Welsh club rugby was enjoying the last of the good old days, not that we were to know it then. Within a couple of years England had established leagues and Anglo-Welsh fixtures had started dying out. In 1990, my first year in senior rugby, the Welsh clubs were themselves forced to accept leagues. By then the pressures had built up on rugby union's fear of professionalism. The advent of the World Cup in 1987 not only led to an explosion in the number of matches played but increased the value of the game commercially. That has worked to the disadvantage of Wales. Our rugby has always been a largely working-class concern, unlike England, Ireland and Scotland where it was more middle class. Attitudes in Wales have always been professional in that rugby has never been just a game, more a way of life, but the small geographical strip from Llanelli in the west to Newport in the east and Ebbw Vale in the north which used to be the strength of Welsh rugby is now its weakness, with too many clubs fighting for too little money.

I never thought of playing rugby union for money. I did, however, become hooked on league and watched Wigan regularly, by now harbouring a threefold ambition: to play for Cardiff, to be capped by Wales and then to turn professional with Wigan. One out of three isn't bad, especially as it is worth more than the other two put together. My first Wales match was as a spectator in 1983 when England came looking for the victory in Cardiff that always eluded them in that era. It did again, although Wales were fortunate to escape with a 13–13 draw.

I was standing on the West Terrace and my most abiding memory of that game is an old man who waved two flags around. When he shoved up England's we all booed, and when he hoisted Wales's there were deafening cheers. My uncle took me down and we got into the ground early to get a position where I could see. I remember the atmosphere, and the noise which built up to a crescendo when Wales ran out. I said to my uncle that one day I wanted to play for Wales at the Arms Park, and it was a goal I never lost sight of. My first cap came in Cardiff, but whereas as a spectator the noise was part of you, and you were part of the noise, as a player you were cocooned in the dressing-room and could only sense the atmosphere. When you emerged from the tunnel, it hit you like a blast of warm air just as when you step out of an air-conditioned aeroplane having landed in a humid country. It is something you have to experience to appreciate fully, and for me no ground will ever compare to the old Arms Park.

As a boy, I was one of thousands hoping to make his fantasy turn into reality. I played for Llantwit Fadre Youth when I was only 14. My cousin, Justin Burnell, was the captain, and I used to go along to their sessions even though I was too young for the team because I enjoyed playing touch rugby with them. I would go on the bus and watch their games, taking things in and learning. I knew some of the boys because they worked for my father, and they were a very strong side. I made my debut for them against Abercynon and scored a try. I then had another year with them before we started to struggle to field a side and I was asked to join Pontypridd Youth along with Paul John. My last year at school had been frustrating, because we had the making of a very strong Pontypridd Schools side with players such as Scott Gibbs, Luc Evans, Rhodri Phillips, my mate Paul Vowles and Jamie Downes but the teachers were in dispute that year and we sat the season out.

One of the teachers apologised to me, but they had a legitimate grievance. They were putting in extra hours to coach sports and were not getting paid for their time, but whereas I was part of a youth team and had a chance to play rugby regularly, other kids were not so fortunate and the cost to the game was probably considerable. I do not blame the teachers for one minute, but at 14 and 15 you are at an impressionable age. With so many pastimes other than rugby, the game undoubtedly lost out. It meant I also missed out on a Wales Schools Under-15 cap, and so when I left school I was determined I would play for Welsh Youth.

Leaving the Llantwit Fadre Youth set-up was a wrench because I had been with the club for all my rugby life. Even now it is still home to me. When I was lining up penalties in Durban's King's Park in the second Test of the Lions' series against South Africa, I took deep breaths and imagined I was back on Cae Fardre, taking practice kicks without a care in the world. I never feel pressure when I am kicking for goal because I am able to blot out the noise and the atmosphere by taking a trip back to my childhood. I have spent hundreds of hours on Cae Fardre (*cae* is the Welsh word for 'field') and I often go back there at times of pressure as a form of therapy, because I always leave relaxed.

Pontypridd was only a few miles away from Llantwit Fadre but it was a different world. The club was one of the top in Welsh rugby, although it had fallen slightly from the heights of the late 1970s when, under Tommy David, they had become one of the best sides in Britain. What struck me very quickly about Ponty was how close-knit the club was. It had, and still has, a strong sense of community, something which a club like Cardiff is not renowned for. I had not been at Pontypridd long when I realised that the shirt I wanted to wear as a man was the black of Ponty, not the blue and black of Cardiff.

Pontypridd have always placed a strong emphasis on their youth side and all our recent internationals have been products of it: Paul John, Martyn Williams, Kevin Morgan, Gareth Wyatt and me. When I made my senior début in 1990, I was already part of the club. If the step up from youth rugby filled me with apprehension, there was no thought of joining another club, and of all the top sides in Wales, none has a better youth structure than Ponty. I had four years in the youth team and won the Welsh Youth cap I coveted. It may be hard to imagine now, but I was quick then and often played on the wing. What happened?

Rugby had taken over my life by then. My mother's washing machine never stopped. If my own and my father's work clothes were not in it, my rugby kit was. I played for the WRU President's Youth XV when I was 16, on the wing. It was an unofficial trial and I was asked to attend a week's training camp in Aberystwyth. I enjoyed the rugby, but the town was boring and when the coaches asked me to spend another week there, I could not face it.

My parents came down to pick me up and I took my father aside, begging him to tell the head coach Brian Nicholas that he needed my help in cutting up buses at work. My mother was not happy but I was soon going home having promised to return the following Thursday to prepare for a trial match. I was chosen to play for the Youth against Welsh Colleges, at outside half, and we beat them for the first time, 24–8. I won my cap against Italy at Waterton Cross at the beginning of 1990. It was a tense, close match which we edged 13–11, and I scored one of our two tries.

I did not play in the next international against France because I was recovering from food poisoning. I was in fact on the bench, praying that I did not have to come on. We lost 26–13 and the next game was against England. My hopes of regaining my place were hit when Pontypridd Youth were banned after having five players sent off in the season. It meant none of us could play for three weeks and we desperately tried to arrange a match the week before the England match, just before the Welsh team was chosen.

The only game we could get was against my old team, Llantwit Fadre, at their ground. The selectors came to watch me and I knew that if I did not perform on my old stamping ground, a place which was as comfortable to me as my bed, I never would. We won comfortably and I landed 10 kicks out of 11. I was chosen to play against England Youth in the unfamiliar surroundings of Wrexham. Rugby may be the national sport of Wales, but soccer has a stranglehold in the north. There was pressure on us to win because we had lost to England that season at every other level. Scott Gibbs was the captain of the side from the centre, and in less than a year we were both to be lining up for our first senior caps – against England!

Scott and I knew each other well. We had played against each other at school and we progressed through the youth ranks together. He was then, as he is now, a very private and quiet person whose detached demeanour off the pitch masks a fierce competitiveness on it. He is a player you are always glad to have on your side. He has a presence and an aura about him, and when he started playing for Neath the following September he made an immediate impact. Although he has since abandoned aspirations to be the captain of Wales, not least because he craves his privacy away from rugby, he leads by example and is someone everyone looks up to, as he showed with the Lions in South Africa.

We salvaged some honour for Wales by defeating England 12–6. I kicked three penalties and dropped a goal in a match which was not much of a spectacle but it was the result which mattered. Although I had by then become a specialist goal-kicker, it was not an aspect of my game that I paid that much attention to. In the summer of that year, after I had made my début for Pontypridd, my uncles Andrew and Peter spent hours with me on the training field to help me develop a style and a rhythm. It was tiring, but they would never let me relent. Their time and their patience helped me become a goal-kicker of international quality and I thought of them after the Lions had won the series in South Africa, uttering a quiet thank you to two top men.

I played two games for Pontypridd that season, against South Wales Police and Bridgend. They had been asking me to have a game most of the season as, having turned 18 the previous summer, I was eligible to play senior rugby. I was apprehensive because I knew that if I failed it would mean a return to junior rugby, and I had set my heart on playing for Wales. What would I do if it turned out that I was not good enough? My father told me not to worry and to get on with it. He is a naturally ebullient character whose motto is 'seize the moment'. When I later received rugby league offers, his advice would always be to take them. I am more like my mother, cautious and emotional. My father has never been bothered when I have received media criticism, even though at times it has been intense and unrelenting. My mother would have happily throttled some of the critics, but to my father it was a case of going out there and proving them wrong. His attitude has always been that you are in charge of your own destiny, not others, and that what matters is not what they say but what you do.

I took the plunge on 14 April 1990. Pontypridd were then coached by Mike Watkins, the former Wales captain and hooker, a larger than life character. The match was at Waterton Cross and we won 18–4. I scored a try, repeating what had become a trend in my débuts for a team, but I did not take any kicks. Two days later, on the Easter Monday, I made my first appearance at Sardis Road. Bridgend were the visitors and they had Robert Howley and Aled Williams at half-back. We defeated them 21–9. I scored a try and landed two kicks, but I did not play for Ponty again that season because I was injured in a youth match.

I had arrived, though, and I knew I was to be part of the squad the following season, which was why I spent the summer preparing for the year I had been waiting for. It was a time of significant change in Welsh rugby because, after years of debate, it was finally agreed that a national league structure would be set up. It meant the end of the old merit-table system which had guaranteed 18 clubs permanent first-class status to the exclusion of all the rest. Clubs like Pontypridd had to give up a lot and their status was no longer guaranteed, but leagues were inevitable. Wales had had two terrible years on the international field, Anglo-Welsh fixtures had virtually ceased to exist because of the English league and it was clear that the Welsh club scene was not preparing players for Test rugby in the way it once had.

It was the moment of truth for me and I spent virtually every spare hour that summer preparing for what lay ahead. It was not quite a leap into the dark, but I did have moments of nervous anxiety, the desire to succeed wrestling with the fear of failure. My aim was to contest for a place in the Pontypridd side, and never in my wildest fantasies did I expect to be lining up for Wales in the New Year. In any sport you need a lucky break, and I was to have mine that September.

CHAPTER THREE

Carface

Pontypridd made me as a player and I will always be in the club's debt. I hope I have paid them something back, not just in terms of points but in helping establish the club as one of the strongest in Wales. From the moment Dennis John joined as coach at the end of 1991, we have always been there at the moment of reckoning, winning the Welsh Cup in 1996 before being crowned champions the following year, my first as captain. I had to miss the closing months of that campaign having broken my arm playing for Wales against England, but the moment we secured the title at Bridgend meant more to me than anything I had achieved in my career, even though I was sitting in the stand. We were not a club with the stature of a Cardiff or a Llanelli; we did not have millionaires waving huge cheques around; and we did not have a succession of top internationals beating a path to our door.

What we had was something money could not buy: an unquenchable spirit and a belief in each other. We were not just players but friends. I have read many times that the characters have gone out of rugby, but they can be found at Sardis Road. The thing that struck me about Pontypridd the day I made my début for them was that it was far more than just a rugby club. Even in the middle of the 1980s, when Ponty had hit lean times and struggled to win matches, they would take busloads of supporters with them to fixtures like London Irish. There is no better-supported club in Wales, and it is no surprise that the Welsh Rugby Union has taken its major A matches to Sardis Road in recent years. When we lost the cup final in 1995, our sense of disappointment as players was all the more acute because we knew we had let the fans down, and we were determined to make it up to them.

After my first game at South Wales Police I was immediately put in my place, as I was ordered to run up and down to the bar getting drinks for the senior players. They were the days when you would play a game and then have a night on the beer. Paul Knight, the Wales prop, was the captain and he would carry the beer kitty in his top pocket. The front row, or 'The Blobs' as we backs called them out of earshot, would go into a huddle and disappear with the cash. It never paid to challenge them.

Pontypridd is not a club where prima donnas last long, and you have to serve your apprenticeship. Everyone looks after each other. In my first full season, we were playing at Pontypool, who were strong then. I had just landed a kick when their number eight, the New Zealander Dean Oswald, clogged me around the head and ran off laughing. Our second row, Steve Bain, chugged after him, telling him to pick on someone his own size. Oswald was quite understandably trying to intimidate a raw 19-year-old, but there were more than a few characters in our side who did not need a second invitation to mix it.

It was the first season of the national league and Pontypridd ensured that the new era for the club game in Wales got off to an explosive start. The campaign started with a couple of friendlies. I played at Nottingham and scored a couple of tries in our 18–17 victory but I was left out against Gloucester the following week at Sardis Road. It was a good game to miss because we were hammered and the first-choice outside half, Andy Phillips, did not have one of his better games. Our opening league game was at Llanelli the following Saturday. I thought I had a chance of being selected but I was apprehensive at training until the team was announced. And then it hit me: Llanelli at Stradey Park, one of rugby's most famous arenas. They had a line-up littered with internationals: Ieuan Evans, Nigel Davies, Phil Davies and Phil May, to name but a few. It took a while to sink in.

Our changing-room before the match was an interesting place to be. Pontypridd at the time had a reputation for being a side which, to put it politely, was not too light on its feet. The previous coaching regime had left after a queue of players found themselves in front of the WRU's disciplinary committee explaining why they had been sent off. It was not difficult to see why we had been in trouble as some players went through their mental routines before the Llanelli game. I sat there goggle-eyed. Some were shouting and screaming, while Denzil Earland, our wing forward, slapped his face so hard that his cheeks turned raw red. I wondered what I had let myself in for, and it was a relief to get out on to the pitch.

There was a huge crowd and no one had given us a chance. There was no cause for anyone to revise their opinion just a minute into the game after Llanelli had nearly scored a try. There was a fracas among the forwards and Les Peard, the international referee, summoned Denzil over. Denzil had given someone a clip and Les told him where the dressing-room was. He had a long walk to the tunnel and the crowd were giving him the bird. Sixty seconds into the first league season and Ponty had written themselves into the record books. Denzil always lived on the edge, and not just on the field, and he will doubtless dine out for many years on the tale of how he became the first player to be sent off in a Welsh national league match.

I received my first set of stitches courtesy of Denzil. We were playing at Glamorgan Wanderers that same season. I tackled an opponent and a ruck formed. I was lying on the floor and received a boot straight in the eye. It was Denzil, confusing me with one of their players. 'Sorry, butt,' he exclaimed as he inspected the damage. It was not a great ground for us: a few years earlier, second row Jim Scarlett had sent through a punch from the middle of a scrum which had connected with his own hooker. The referee spotted the deed and, as the hooker lay poleaxed on the ground, ordered Jim off, a real double whammy. Jim was also to have his moment of notoriety at Stradey Park. As I was being stitched up, the doctor had an attack of the shakes and I thought he was going to poke the needle straight into my eye. Thanks, Denzil!

Denzil was a top guy when he was not trying to kick your head off, a hard man nobody took liberties with. He was from Maerdy in the Rhondda, a tough area where the life expectancy of parked cars is not long. The story is that Denzil used to park his car without bothering to even lock it. Not that it was ever nicked. He would put his photograph in the back window, the mildest of hints at what reprisals would follow. He was not someone to get on the wrong side of.

Without him at Llanelli, it was surely a case of how many we could hold them to. They were putting pressure on our line shortly after Denzil's departure but we managed to force a drop-out. I took it quickly and one of the forwards hacked the ball downfield. Ieuan tried to kick it into touch but Jim Scarlett charged his clearance down and prop Nigel Bezani claimed the try as the ball rolled over their line. We started to believe in miracles and desperation crept into Llanelli's play.

We felt reasonably confident at half-time, but no sooner had the second period started than Les was reaching into his pocket again. Phil May killed the ball in a ruck and Jim decided to do something about it. Ball-killing was a speciality in those days. Players like Phil and Cardiff's Bob Lakin were prepared to take kickings galore in order to prevent the opposition from getting the ball. Bob's claim to fame is that he had more than 200 stitches inserted into various head wounds during his career. Phil took a slippering that day, Jim mistaking his body for a trampoline. Les sent him to the showers and I could not believe it. Taking Llanelli on with 15 men was hard enough, but to try it with 13 was suicide.

Jim trudged forlornly off. He was always in trouble with referees, but off the field he was a gentle man. He came into rugby late, having been a basketball player, and his natural athleticism made up for his lack of inches as a second row. He was not a particularly dirty player but he gained a reputation quickly and that, together with his distinctive appearance, flowing dark hair which made him look like an Indian brave, meant his chances of getting away with any nonsense were virtually zero. Later that season we were playing Swansea at home and Jim lost a line-out on our own throw. They moved it wide and we just managed to stop them in the corner. I felt someone pick me off the ground. It was Jim. 'Sorry, Neil,' he said. 'I am just having a nightmare.' And he was off. That was Jim, an enigma. A shy character, he was misunderstood. Had it not been for his disciplinary record, he would probably have gone all the way to the top. Some players get away with a lot, others do not. Jim had the misfortune to fall into the latter category and he sadly faded out of the game.

The minutes which followed Jim's dismissal were probably the most significant in my career. We were looking down the barrel and Llanelli came at us with fresh purpose. They launched an attack which seemed certain to end in a try, but Nigel Davies, the

Wales centre who was to become a great friend of mine, threw out a wild pass near our twenty-two. I picked the ball up and was off. Space opened up in front of me and, showing a turn of speed, I scored under the posts. Jonathan Mason was taking the goal-kicks then, so it was my one contribution to the scoreboard and it ensured that, as well as getting a highly improbable 10–10 draw, the headlines were not all about the two players who had been sent off.

Outside half is a position in Wales which is held to have mystical qualities. When you pull on the Welsh number ten jersey, you are made only too aware of the greats in whose footsteps you are treading. Much was made of my try at Llanelli and suddenly, in the eyes of the media, a new star was born. I was not getting carried away, but it was a strange sensation to go from being a nobody one day to being the most talked-about player in Wales the next. Not that the Pontypridd players were going to let my head swell. What was significant about Llanelli was not my try but that we held on against one of the top clubs in Wales despite being two men short. Mike Watkins was asked afterwards how he intended to celebrate the achievement. 'We will have a few beers and probably come home on Tuesday,' he replied.

Spike, as he is known to everyone involved in the Welsh game, stood down as coach at the end of the season, but he played a major role in my development as a player. He did not take any messing, but he was a player-orientated coach who protected his squad. I have been fortunate to have had quality coaching throughout my career, starting with Dennis John. Mike Mawn and Rhys Lewis were the Pontypridd Youth coaches, Spike and Les Brown were in charge at Pontypridd before the arrival of Dennis and Lynn Howells, and I have played under four coaches at national level: Ron Waldron, Alan Davies, Alex Evans and Kevin Bowring, all different characters and tacticians and all with so much to offer players. I have always relished training and I have never had any problem adjusting to a new coach – which is probably just as well given the tendency of Wales to fire and hire in times of strife.

We had a reasonable first season in the league but we did not beat enough of the top sides. I took over the kicking duties after Jonathan Mason said he had had enough. I played in 14 league matches and scored 127 points, including five tries, and I suppose it said something of the state of the Welsh game at the time that following my performance at Llanelli I was being tipped as a Wales outside half of the future. Within two months I was playing for the WRU President's Select Under-21s against the *Rugby News* New Zealanders at Sardis Road. It was not a representative match and in no way could they be described as the All Black Under-21s, but no team from New Zealand is easy to beat and we turned on the style in defeating them 34–13. I scored 14 points with the boot and Paul John, who was then playing for Cardiff, claimed one of our five tries. Following the success of the Wales Schools Under-18 team in New Zealand that summer, the medium-term future for Wales looked bright.

Six of the Under-21 side went on to be capped by Wales and the following month I was chosen to play for Wales B against the Netherlands in Leiden. Paul John was again my half-back partner – Robert Howley was on the bench – and Steele Lewis, one of the Pontypridd centres, was in the side. Stella toured Australia with Wales in 1991 but was never to win a cap, although he was very close on more than one occasion. He, along with Phil John, Greg Prosser, Mark Rowley and Dale McIntosh of the current Ponty-pridd squad, epitomises the ethos of the club.

Stella was the one who after my début at Waterton Cross ensured that I acted as bar waiter that night. I came through the youth ranks with his brother, Jason, and they are both firm friends of mine. Stella may play in the centre but there is nothing soft about him. He relishes the physical side of the game and is phenomenally strong. The Dutch did not know what had hit them that December day because Stella was partnered in the midfield by Scott Gibbs, who had made a big name for himself in three months at Neath. Ron Waldron, the Neath team manager, was the Wales coach in 1990 and there was a big Neath influence in Holland. I had no quarrel with that because Neath were by far and away the strongest club in Wales. They had the inaugural league title wrapped up by Christmas, although we had given them their biggest fright a week before the Holland game when we held them to 28–27 at the Gnoll, a match we should have won having outscored them on tries.

We beat the Dutch easily and attention then turned to the Five Nations Championship, which was only six weeks away. My name was being canvassed in the media but I did not hold out any great hopes. David Evans, the Cardiff outside half, had played for Wales against the Barbarians in October while Adrian Davies of Neath was on the bench, Colin Stephens was making a name for himself at Llanelli having succeeded Jonathan Davies the previous year and Aled Williams had been capped in the summer. All four were more classical Welsh outside halves than me: David was a deceptive runner; Adrian was a footballer of rare ability, a natural ball-player who played with an effortless ease; there was a touch of Phil Bennett about Colin, with his dazzling pace off the mark which made him such a dangerous counter-attacker; and Aled was similar to Colin, quick to exploit a gap, an exciting player who was to become an important part of a successful Swansea side. I was probably a better defender than the other four and a more consistent kicker but, with Paul Thorburn, who was the Wales captain, one of the best goal-kickers in the international game at the time, I knew that the outside half who played against England would be the one whom Ron considered to be the most complete player in the position. While I lived in hope, I never expected to be chosen in the squad, let alone the team, but time was on my side and my priority was still proving myself with Pontypridd.

On the day the squad was announced I was working with my father, loading a skip. He told me he was slipping away for a few minutes to grab some sandwiches. I presumed he was going off to the pub, a suspicion which was confirmed when he came back later with a big grin on his face. He told me I had been chosen in the Wales squad. I did not believe it and asked him what he had been drinking. He insisted, but I would have gone on thinking he was winding me up had he not brought a newspaper back with him. The print did not lie: my name was there, along with Stella's and those of Pontypridd's props Neil Eynon and Paul Knight. Scott Gibbs was also included: our careers had run in parallel lines since we were at school and now we were poised to step on to the biggest stage of all. I still did not think I would play against England, but I had arrived, less than eight years from the day when I had stood on the West Terrace of the Arms Park and vowed to a nodding uncle that I would one day be back there as a player. That moment was nigh.

CHAPTER FOUR

Up and Under

The Welsh squad met on a Sunday at Sophia Gardens in Cardiff for a five-day training camp to prepare for the Five Nations. The team to face England was to be announced that Thursday, but before we touched a rugby ball we were sent on a series of runs. Ron Waldron had enlisted Brian Roper, the marathon runner, as his fitness coach and our first task was a five-mile race followed by five laps of the rugby field. The Neath players were used to Ron and they were up at the front with Brian on the run which took us around Cardiff Castle and alongside the River Taff. I felt like jumping in and ended up plodding with the backmarkers, knackered by the time we started going through rugby routines.

That was Ron's way. He had helped turn Neath around from being one of the weaker sides in the Merit Table to a club which was feared throughout Britain. When he took over as Wales coach midway through the 1990 championship campaign, it was inevitable he would turn to those players he knew and trusted. The same was to happen in 1995 when Alex Evans, Cardiff's rugby director, became Wales's coach for the World Cup campaign. Neath had based their game on fitness, speed and support. Many Welsh clubs were set-piece-orientated and they were not able to live with the ferocious energy of Neath's game. Few teams came away from the Gnoll with anything better than a 40-point hiding.

Ron's problem was that success at club level was one thing, but international rugby was a completely different ball game. What his time with Wales showed was that our club rugby had declined markedly from even ten years before. I would constantly read comments from people in England that they could not understand why Wales were struggling in the championship. They would watch the highlights of a top club game on *Rugby Special* every week and say that it compared favourably with anything England had to offer, especially in terms of competitiveness and passion. What they could not appreciate was that it was a case of like against like, that Welsh rugby had become so parochial that when we were exposed to outside influences we struggled. We were no longer a self-sufficient rugby nation.

Ron had no chance of reversing the decline. He had been appointed two matches into the 1990 championship after John Ryan had resigned suddenly following a record defeat at Twickenham. Ryan had taken over from Tony Gray in the summer of 1988 after Wales had suffered a humiliating tour of New Zealand. Flying high in April when he was named European coach of the year after guiding Wales to their first Triple Crown for nine years, Gray was shot down in May, a dreadful decision by the WRU who seemed to believe that in 1987 Wales were the third best side in the world, whereas their play-off victory against Australia merely meant they were third in the World Cup. They conveniently forgot that New Zealand had defeated us in the semi-final 49–6. Even though Wales had declined from the heights of the 1970s, there was no sense of realism. Coaches were expected to wave a magic wand or make way for another conjurer.

Ron's reign was to end ignominiously in Australia in the summer of 1991, his reputation in tatters, but I rated him highly as a coach. His ideas were sound but he did not have the players. It was one thing for Neath to sweep all before them in Wales, but the likes of England, France and Australia, who all defeated us convincingly that year, were playing at a far higher standard. That was the thing which struck me when I made my début against England: it was so different from the Welsh club game, not just in terms of atmosphere and the size of the crowd, but in the power of the England eight, the organisation of their backs and their proficiency as a team. We gave our all and defended bravely, but it was not a contest of equals.

Yet Ron ended up being judged on the past rather than the present, like so many players, and coaches, before and after him.

The WRU's response to the New Zealand tour had encouraged a fresh exodus of players to rugby league; Jonathan Davies, who had succeeded Gareth Davies as my hero, was the most grievous loss. John Devereux and David Young, two of the Welsh 1989 Lions, followed, and we were to lose players of the quality of Allan Bateman, Scott Gibbs and Scott Quinnell. I very nearly went to rugby league myself. Had Wigan come in for me, I am sure I would have gone. The WRU did not seem to be facing up to the demands of a fast-changing game and Welsh rugby became a state of fast-flowing despair.

Not that I thought about that when my name was read out in the team to face England. I had only played 15 matches for Pontypridd. When Ron spoke my name, a knot formed in my throat and I burst into tears. A few of us had gone out on the town the night before to celebrate the end of training, and when we tried to get into our rooms at the National Sports Centre we found we were locked out. Someone spotted an open window a couple of floors up at the back of the building and we clambered on to a flat roof to get in. A hoover was lying around and it was plugged in and left whirring outside Ron's room. There were a few other antics and I expected us to get a roasting at breakfast, but Ron said nothing. If he did know who was responsible, he never held it against us.

It took a long time to sink in. Just three years before, I had stood on the East Terrace cheering Wales on their way to the Triple Crown, shouting for players like Ieuan Evans, Mark Ring, Paul Thorburn and Robert Jones. And here I was, still a teenager and in the same side as them. Scott Gibbs was also picked and two nervous 19-year-olds shared a room when we gathered as a squad three days before the international at the National Stadium. Scott is more laid-back than me. I tend to wear my heart on my sleeve, and as the hours to the kick-off ticked away, the butterflies in my stomach bred rapidly.

We were staying at the Angel Hotel, across the road from the ground. We walked the few yards to the National Stadium carrying our bags. I had strolled along Westgate Street many times, but this was completely different: I was on a date with destiny. I have found the atmosphere in Cardiff on international day unlike that in any other country, not least because the ground is unique in that it is in the centre of the city. We had tried to take it easy the day before the match, but you could not get away from what was taking place the following afternoon. Playing for the Llantwit Fadre mini-section seemed a world away. Then you carried only the hopes of your parents; a nation now expected.

Even though Wales had won only one of their previous nine championship matches, there was still a belief throughout the country. That success had come against England in 1989, when Wales were trying to avoid the whitewash and the English were going for the championship. They were again undone by their poor record in Cardiff, a ground they had last won at in 1963, but they were a different proposition in 1991. They had been unlucky not to win the Grand Slam the previous year when their reward for some enterprising rugby was to see Scotland take the championship from them.

England tightened up in 1991. They had the nucleus of the 1989 Lions pack which had got the better of Australia and they had a potent back-line which included Will Carling, Jeremy Guscott, Rory Underwood and Rob Andrew. Manager Geoff Cooke was determined to avoid a repeat of 1989, and as England travelled into Wales by coach he played at full blast a tape of the Arms Park crowd singing the national anthem. They stayed in a hotel opposite ours and they too walked to the ground. Cooke made his players confront their demons and it was clear from the start of the game that they were not going to be weighed down by the burden of history. They played with a ruthless professionalism, and although we contained them to just one try, Simon Hodgkinson kicked seven penalties to sink us.

We warmed up in those days at the back of the ground in our trainers. You were shielded from the noise inside the stadium and when you ran out on to the pitch your eardrums exploded. There was so much to take in, a sea of red and white, and I looked in vain for familiar faces. My girlfriend, Cathryn, had asked for an East Terrace ticket. It was where she always stood and she did not want to go into the stand just because I was playing. My father was there but my mother stayed at home. She has hardly ever watched me play for Wales, but she has been a regular at Pontypridd. She often goes to see Llantwit Fadre and it was only when we played France at the Arms Park the following year thatshe grew agitated for a ticket. It was not me who was the draw, however, but Philippe Sella, the French centre who was her favourite player! I told my parents that if I was selected to go to South Africa with the Lions in 1997 I would pay for them both to follow the tour, but even then my mother took some persuading to go. She is afraid of being overcome by the emotion of the moment, and as I stood singing the Welsh national anthem along with the crowd before the start of the England international, I knew why some players cried at that point. It was a very moving experience.

I have an excellent recollection of most of the matches I have played in, but England 1991 is a blur. I remember that my first tackle was on flanker Peter Winterbottom and that I sliced my first kick to touch so badly that number eight Dean Richards caught the ball in midfield. He was so surprised that he knocked it on. We were under a lot of pressure, but we did have some chances. Paul Thorburn had one of those rare days when his boot failed him and he ended up calling on me to kick a penalty which earned me my first points for Wales. England clinched their first win in Cardiff for 28 years 25–6 and there was no question that they were the better side. The scoreline should have been closer but they were on their way to the Grand Slam.

I felt reasonably pleased with my performance. Their forwards had been on top and there was no way we could influence the game from behind. Ron and his fellow selectors chose the same team for the international against Scotland at Murrayfield two weeks later. We were taken apart up front and were well beaten 32–12. We showed what we were capable of in the backs by creating a superb try for the wing Steve Ford, but I had far more work to do in defence than in attack. Scotland were strong then: seven of their players had toured with the 1989 Lions and they were well drilled. The writing was on the wall for us and I was starting to learn that people built you up to knock you down. Ron had been declared the Messiah 12 months before, but fingers were now pointing and changes had to be made for the Ireland match.

Brian Williams lost his place at prop. He was a player who symbolised the Neath game. Although he was no more than 14 stone, he held his place in the Neath front row and was a rampant player in the loose, formidably strong in the maul. He summed up Ron's plight: Brian's was a popular selection when he was drafted into the Wales team immediately after Ron's appointment. He represented a move away from the set-piece strategy of Ryan to the more dynamic game perfected by Neath, but while he was not found out as a scrummager in the Welsh club game, there was no hiding place on the international scene. As he became worn down in the tight, his loose play inevitably suffered. Ron was forced to compromise his principles by turning to the scrummaging prop he had discarded, Mike Griffiths, and it was at that moment (with the benefit of hindsight) that the Neath experiment came to grief.

We drew with Ireland in Cardiff in an open, error-strewn game between two teams who had forgotten how to win. I dropped a goal and scored a try, but it was a match we threw away. When I was first chosen to play for Wales, Spike took me to one side and said to do my own thing and not to worry about what anyone might say, and I was determined to enjoy international rugby. Ireland gave me my first chance to show what I could do as an outside half and I made some telling breaks. I have heard it said many times over the years that I have only played for Wales because of my goal-kicking, but when I broke into the side Paul Thorburn was the kicker. I was selected because of my play as an outside half. The kicking came later.

We finished the championship at the Parc des Princes, where Serge Blanco was in his pomp. It was his last Five Nations match and he marked the occasion by scoring an 80-yard try in the opening minutes. It was typically outrageous and he finished the move off by kicking the ball to our try-line. It bobbled for 30 yards along the touchline, never once deviating from its chosen course, and it settled nicely for the peerless full-back to fall on it. We were again destroyed up front and France had far too much pace and flair for us behind. All their three-quarters scored tries and all we could muster in reply was a solitary penalty from Paul. It was always going to be a damage-limitation exercise for us. We had not won in Paris for 16 years and France exploited our vulnerability from the outset. They have always played with a curious mixture of beauty and brutality, the types who smile at you and then head-butt you. They put it about and turn it on and you have to stand toe-to-toe with them.

Pontypridd did that in the Heineken Cup in the 1997–98 season and it led to the battle of Brive, but that is another story. We were hopelessly outclassed in Paris in 1991 and finished a distant second. We failed to win a championship match for the second season in a row and next up was a tour to Australia, who had emerged as the strongest country in the world. As was the case in

New Zealand in 1988, we were going to the wrong place at the wrong time. Morale was poor and, while you always have to be positive, we knew we were going to be up against it with matches against Queensland and New South Wales as well as the Wallabies.

Wales had tried the big-pack approach under John Ryan and it had failed. So, too, had Ron's attempt to make the Neath model work. You could feel tension mounting in the squad, a tension which was to explode at the end of the Australia tour. Much as I admired Ron, he had no answer when his attempt to make Wales a mobile, ball-handling side foundered on the huge packs we came up against. Ron came to be savaged in the media, the same media which had fêted his appointment. He had done what he had said he would do; that it failed was not, ultimately, his fault. He, like Ryan before him, was not in control of his own destiny. Wales were paying for the failure to invest in the success of the 1970s and were being left behind.

But, even in those amateur days, the search was for scapegoats, not answers. The reason he had been brought in was also the reason he left: poor results. He stood down after suffering ill-health on his return home from Australia, but there is no way he would have survived what was one of the most sorry sagas in the proud history of Welsh rugby. A year which had started with me feeling on top of the world crumbled around me as I found myself shaking hands with both of the twin impostors, triumph and disaster, within the space of six months. The World Cup was being held that autumn, but my aspirations of being part of what had become one of the biggest events in sport ended in Australia. I flew there with my career on the up and returned down, very down.

CHAPTER FIVE

Bushwhacked

My first season in senior rugby had been a roller-coaster ride. I had started out with the aim of becoming Ponty-pridd's regular outside half, something I knew I could not take for granted. Yet I ended it as Wales's first-choice number ten. At times I had to pinch myself because it was so hard to believe, but the year had shown me that you needed a thick skin if you were to survive what was a turbulent period. The more the defeats mounted, the more the players of the 1970s were wheeled out to say what an awful bunch their successors were.

Criticism has never bothered me. I have used it as a form of therapy, a way of keeping my motivation level high. Other players are badly affected by what others say and write about them. My view is that you have to accept praise when it is offered and take the stick when things are going badly – and how the mud flew when we returned from Australia. We had brought it upon ourselves: dreadfully lacking on the field, we shamed the nation in the after-match function at Ballymore following our hammering by the Wallabies.

When the squad gathered before flying out, I felt confident. Pontypridd had finished in the top half of the premier division and, although we made an early exit from the cup after losing at home to Llanelli, we knew we were good enough to compete with the best in Wales. We would have finished third had we not had another player sent off when we were leading 18–15 at Swansea. My half-back partner, Robert Davies, saw red after some indelicate footwork, and they sneaked home by three points. It is still a ground where I have not been on the winning side in a club match.

If the future looked good for Pontypridd, the Welsh players knew we were up against it going to Australia. Our first stop was Cottisloe, a resort just outside Perth, and it set the tone for the tour. The beds in the hotel were damp and it was clear that the manager, Clive Rowlands, and Ron were not going to get on. Their differences were graphically exposed when Clive's son-in-law, scrum half Robert Jones, one of our few world-class players, was left out of the Test team. As it became clear that we not only had no chance of winning the Test but were not even going to make a game of it, the players started falling out. With Clive and Ron not getting on, there was nobody to step in to sort it out, and seldom can the Australians have been so glad to see the back of a group of tourists. Our ship was rudderless and, not surprisingly, it sank like a stone.

We got off to a winning start in Perth against Western Australia. It was a city where rugby union meant little to the locals. Aussie Rules had just taken off in a big way and the state side had been fortified by a group of New Zealanders, one of whom, flanker Robert Edwards, had played for Cross Keys. We laboured our way to a 22–6 victory and did not impress the watching Wallaby spies. I sat on the bench because Adrian Davies was chosen at outside half, and he was to remain in the position the following week against the far stronger Queensland. We performed respectably that day, recovering from a half-time deficit of 23–6 to 26–24 with a conversion to come late on, but they pulled ahead at the death to win 35–24. It was a defeat, but against a side packed with internationals, including 12 who were to be involved in the Test two weeks later, it was not a disgrace.

We followed it up with a midweek victory against ACT in Canberra. It was my first appearance of the tour and the game was played in terrible conditions. It had been raining for days and the pitch had been ploughed up by two warm-up matches which were amazingly allowed to go ahead. I kicked a penalty, the only score of the second half, to help us to a 7–3 victory after number eight Sean Legge had scored the only try of the game. It was a notable victory, even if ACT were not the force then that they are now in the Super 12. Three matches into the tour, we had won two and given Queensland a fright: no obvious sign of the horrors to come.

The picture changed at Concord Oval where we faced a New South Wales team of all the talents which had not lost that year and was to go through the whole season unbeaten. They went at us from the start and it was like being hit by a hurricane. I was playing at outside half and it was my chance to stake a claim for the Test berth. Some chance. They were 39–0 up at half-time and we only seemed to touch the ball to kick off. They lost two of their best players in the first half, scrum half Nick Farr-Jones and rampaging flanker Willie Ofahengaue, but it made no difference. They already had the game won and the pair were holding themselves back for the Test match.

Their power, angles of running and support play were too much for us. We missed any number of first-time tackles and it was boys against men. We scored two tries late on, but they were not even by way of consolation. We conceded 13 tries and lost 71–8, a score which would be 84–10 under today's scoring values. No one said anything afterwards. A nation had lost to a province in a depressingly one-sided contest. The international against Australia, who were to field nine of the New South Wales side, was only seven days away but there was only one place we wanted to be: home.

I was left out of the Test side and I had no complaints, although I was disappointed not to be on the bench. Adrian captained the midweek side to a 35–7 victory over Queensland Country Origin and he had not had a bad tour. He scored three of our six points in the international with his fifth drop goal of the tour, but he was swamped like the rest of the men in red by a tidal wave of green and gold. We were crushed 63–6, the worst ever defeat suffered by one of the eight major nations in world rugby. We were a divided and dispirited bunch, a poor advert for the Welsh game – but there was worse to come.

The after-match function at Ballymore was an informal affair, unlike the stuffy, dinner-jacket junkets which follow Five Nations matches. Women were invited and the idea was for the players to spend a couple of hours together before having the night to spend as they wished. I was struck by the professionalism of the Australian squad: they were all sipping orange juice or mineral water. Not one of them touched a drop of alcohol. They may have had a match against England the following week, but I know that in the same position we would have been getting the beer down our necks.

The food had not long been served when the bread rolls and miniature rugby balls started flying. Beer had been consumed very quickly and its effects showed. There was a lot of shouting and swearing and the Australians were looking at us, shaking their heads in disbelief. Some of the women complained but it made no difference. I tried to keep my head down and concentrate on eating but the evening deteriorated even further. A group of players had an argument and a scuffle broke out. The row was over speaking to journalists. Some of the Neath contingent, loyal to Ron to the last, did not want anyone bad-mouthing him, and they tried to gag those they felt wanted to see him replaced and who were prepared to say so publicly.

They knew that Ron was not going to survive and that some senior players were saying that they were considering retiring from international rugby, but in their attempts to protect him, all they ensured was that he had absolutely no chance of surviving once we returned home. I did not see the scuffle, but the centre Mike Hall was led away for stitches after a glass shattered in his hand. I heard a woman crying and we were hustled on to the bus to be taken back to our hotel. It was a terrible way to behave and that pathetic spectacle was to be reported around the world, quite rightly. We were all deflated after two humiliating defeats, but to behave in a manner lacking even the most basic courtesy was unforgivable. Clive and Ron had been warned by the Australian RFU's liaison officer that things were about to boil over, but nothing was done. We let down not only ourselves but our nation and I was surprised that the Australians were prepared to have us back five years later.

Even though I was not involved in the trouble, my behaviour that tour left a considerable amount to be desired, and I returned home a sadder but a much wiser man. I had been undisciplined, drinking too much and staying out late. We were like a pub side, not an international team, and it was small wonder that I was dropped from the Test side. I was not worth my place. My attitude stank. Perhaps I had had too much too soon, but the Australians had shown me the way forward. I brought back some of their tactics to Pontypridd and we were to use them to good effect in the coming years, but more than that I appreciated that if you were to become a top international you had to set yourself high standards both on and off the field.

The tour had started badly for me because I was desperately homesick and I never really focused on the rugby. I did not even bother to ask Ron why he had dropped me from the Test team. It was as if I didn't care. All I wanted to do was get home and start afresh. I thought again about switching to rugby league, and Warrington expressed an interest in me. They offered an easy way out. I had won four Wales caps and I was not likely to be involved in the World Cup that year. Why not take the money and run?

I could understand why some of the experienced players were thinking about packing in the international game. We were hosting a pool in the World Cup, but Australia were among the teams in our group and we were hardly going to turn things around in a couple of months. When I had been selected to play for Wales against England I had felt so much pride that I wanted to tell the whole world, but we had flown back into Heathrow with heads bowed, not wanting to speak to anyone. There had been more scenes on the plane home and the media were waiting for us in numbers, cameras flashing, notebooks poised. We were like criminals who had been extradited from a foreign country and there was no 'welcome home' party waiting for us back in Wales. We had brought disgrace upon Welsh rugby and you did not have to have an Oxbridge degree to know that changes were going to be made.

A few days after we got back, the WRU summoned the players for an individual chat. They wanted to find out exactly what had happened in Australia. Ron was taken to hospital shortly after he returned home. He had a blood clot on his lung and he resigned as coach and team manager because of his health. He would not have been kept on anyway, however, because he had been in charge of a hopelessly divided squad. Ron was an honest man who did his best. He was let down in the end by the system and by some of the players in Australia. Paul Thorburn retired from international rugby and issued an emotional statement supporting Ron, but it was too late for that.

I will always be grateful to Ron because he gave me my chance. Had the standard of club rugby in Wales been higher at the time of his appointment, and had other club coaches shared his vision of the game, perhaps he would have been more successful – not that we would have had a chance in Australia, though. I had never felt there was much of a division between the Neath players and the rest of us. I tended to get on with everyone, but perhaps I was too inexperienced to read between the lines. It was my first major tour, and the only one I have not enjoyed. There I was in a country of astonishing scenery and variety and I was looking forward to going home. I have never made that mistake again, and in 1996 I had the fortune of going back to Australia with Wales. We may not have been appreciably better as a rugby team, although we were more competitive, but we made sure that we did not abuse the excellent hospitality we received. I would like to think that the 1996 squad went some way to making up for the excesses and the failings of the 1991 visitors.

Tony Gray, the coach Wales had sacked after the 1988 New Zealand tour, was expected to be Ron's temporary successor. His job was to be to pilot the team through the World Cup group. That meant defeating Argentina and Western Samoa, because we knew Australia were going to be too strong for us. Gray was nominated by the executive committee of the WRU but, in a rare show of defiance, the general committee refused to rubber-stamp the appointment, even though Gray was a member of that august body, and instead asked Alan Davies to take over the role on a caretaker basis.

Although he was born in Wales, Davies had made his name in England, where he had helped take Nottingham from obscurity into the first division. He had coached England A and he had taken the full England squad on a tour down under in 1988. The obvious advantage he had, apart from his international experience, was that he would not take up the job with labels stuck all over him.

John Ryan had been a coach of Newport and was seen as having a bias towards Gwent rugby. Letter columns during his reign were full of unhelpful advice from supporters in West Wales; the east took its revenge after Ron's appointment. Davies did not come carrying any baggage with him and, on paper, he appeared to be the ideal man to heal what had become a gaping wound. I have often wondered since why he took it on: the post was unpaid and, if it could be said that he had nothing to lose because we were a laughing stock, what chance did he have of being successful?

He was to leave me out of his first squad, one of ten players who had gone to Australia who were deemed surplus to requirements, but I had only just turned 20 and, while I was naturally disappointed, I was not dispirited. Only four Neath players remained in the squad. Another dream had died.

CHAPTER SIX

Centre Stage

I took a long, hard look at myself in the weeks after the tour of Australia and I did not like what I saw. I should have been part of Wales's World Cup squad, but instead of facing the Wallabies I was rubbing shoulders with the likes of Brixham and Lydney. I had no one to blame but myself and I spent the weeks leading up to the new season working on all aspects of my game, particularly goal-kicking. The retirement of Paul Thorburn meant that Wales had to replace him as an accumulator of points. Mark Ring, the Cardiff centre, was chosen by Alan Davies as his first outside half and goal-kicker.

Ringo was one of the most naturally talented players of his era and he would have gone on a Lions tour but for two serious knee injuries. He played most of his rugby for Cardiff in the centre, where his outrageous tricks made him the darling of the crowd, but he always hankered after a return to the position he had played in youth rugby – outside half. He had missed the tour of Australia because Ron had feared Ringo's knees would not stand up to the hard grounds, and the pity for him was that when Alan gave him a chance at number ten he was not fully fit. He soldiered on through the World Cup campaign but hardly played again that season. Wales would need both a goal-kicker and an outside half for the Five Nations.

I was determined to do well for Pontypridd, but we started the league programme in the bottom gear and failed to get going. We lost our opening game against Llanelli despite leading 16–3 with 20 minutes to go and were then beaten at newly promoted Newport. Spike had quit as coach for reasons which were never made plain and his assistant, Les Brown, took over. Les was a smashing bloke but he struggled to impose his authority on the squad and the senior players did what they wanted. There was too much messing about in training and it showed in our results. We were fortunate there was no relegation that season, because we slid to the foot of the table with just one victory.

The turning point came just before Christmas when Dennis John, who had been coaching the reserve team at Cardiff, replaced Les. I had known Dennis since I was seven when I started playing mini-rugby at Llantwit Fadre. His son, Paul, had left Cardiff earlier in the year and we had resumed our half-back partnership. Our families had gone on holidays together, but there were to be no personal favours from Dennis. He had played rugby at a high level as a scrum half with Pontypool and Pontypridd and he was the man we needed at Ponty.

You felt the difference in his first training session. There was no more messing around. He brought Lynn Howells with him to coach the forwards but he did not recruit any new players. He told us that, as long as we applied ourselves and recognised our ability as individuals and as a team, he had no need to. His first match in charge was the traditional Boxing Day derby against the club he had just left, Cardiff, at the Arms Park. We turned them over 27–10 and a new era in the history of Pontypridd had started.

We won our next six league matches and had a chance of winning the title when we went to Swansea, but, not for the first or the last time, our hopes were to founder at a ground where we always seem to be at our worst. We held them in the first half, but after the interval they turned on the style and thrashed us 46–12 on their way to the title. We finished third in the table, one point behind Llanelli, a notable achievement after our wretched start. I was the top scorer in the first division with 173 points and we also made the semi-finals of the Welsh Cup – a day when I made the headlines for all the wrong reasons – and since then we have always been in the chase for silverware.

While Wales were taking part in the World Cup, I was involved with the Wales Under-21s. A few days after the shock defeat to Western Samoa which effectively ended our hopes of making the knock-out stage of the tournament, I was at Rodney Parade for the Under-21 international against Ireland. Kevin Bowring, who was later to succeed Alan Davies, was the Under-21 coach, and if the experience of not being part of rugby's biggest tournament was a chastening one, Kevin was a coach who believed in giving his players freedom of expression. I thrived under him and we played well to defeat the Irish 22–15. Robert Howley was my scrum half, the beginning of a partnership which was to flourish.

After Wales's early elimination from the World Cup, Alan Davies said he did not want to become the coach on a permanent basis because he did not believe he had the strength of character to bear the hopes of a nation when the structure of the Welsh game was not supporting the players. I had not met him at that stage, but the players in the squad I spoke to were unanimous in wanting him to stay on. Alan was part of a strong team: Gareth Jenkins, the innovative and passionate Llanelli coach, was his assistant, while Bob Norster, the former Wales second row and captain, was the manager. Fortunately, all three were persuaded to stay on.

Despite the disappointments of losing to Western Samoa and Australia, the three had gone a long way to repairing the hearts and minds of the players, which had fallen into a desperate state of disrepair after the traumas of the previous three years. With Ringo's knees giving out after the World Cup, I knew there was going to be a new outside half in the championship. David Evans, Adrian Davies, Colin Stephens and Aled Williams were all in the running, but by now my goal-kicking had become consistent and I was confident of at least making the squad.

Colin Stephens was to succeed Ringo at outside half, the eighth player to be tried in the position in the three years since Jonathan Davies had left for rugby league, after Bleddyn Bowen, Paul Turner, Tony Clement, David Evans, me, Adrian Davies and Mark Ring. A peculiarity of the Welsh game is that, no matter how the national team is faring, the outside half is always judged on the legends who have worn the jersey in the past. Colin was not to see the season out. His successor was me.

The decision of Alan Davies and his fellow selectors to play me in the centre, even though I had never played there in my senior career, brought an end to my short career as a tiler. Any misgivings I felt about playing out of position were swept away by relief and elation. The dejection of the previous summer had given way to a sense of optimism. When I gathered with the squad, the difference in morale was obvious: no more cliques or suspicious minds. We were as one again, off to Dublin in search of our first championship victory of the decade.

I took to Alan Davies immediately. He had a quiet air about him and was not easily ruffled, but he was also competitive. He had not taken on the Wales job, giving up his job and home in Nottingham, just for something to do. He had left the mining village of Ynysybwl, a couple of punts away from Pontypridd, when he was ten, and the Welshness that had lain dormant in him since then surfaced when he got a feel for the passion and history of our game.

He was in the end to find himself sacrificed, like others before him, for failings other than his own, but he, together with Bob Norster and Gareth Jenkins, should be given credit for helping the Wales team regain respectability. By the time they had been shown the door in 1995, it had been forgotten just how poor we were between 1988 and 1991, just how low we had sunk. We were rock bottom, and the fact that we have struggled since their departure shows that it was not they who were lacking, but those who oversaw them.

We won two matches out of four in the 1992 championship, Wales's best year since 1988. We should have made it three but we showed France too much respect in Cardiff. Dublin was a special moment, the first time many of us had tasted a Five Nations victory. Stuart Davies, the Swansea number eight who was making his début, scored our try and we edged home 16–15 in a fixture which the home side has won only twice since 1982. When we had to find a new home in 1997 because of the reconstruction of the National Stadium, I would not have minded Lansdowne Road being chosen as our temporary base. I have never lost at the ground, and I have never been on the winning side against Ireland in Cardiff.

The only side which outclassed us that year was England. We were whitewashed 24–0, the first time Wales had failed to score a point in the championship for 22 years. We were overpowered at forward and it was a purely defensive operation. However, the side which had leaked 13 tries to New South Wales and 12 to Australia was no longer a pushover. Only five tries were scored against us that championship. The coaches concentrated on our defensive organisation, and if we were not a potent attacking force, it was a case of learning to walk again before we dared run.

As Newcastle United found out under Kevin Keegan, attack and defence go together. We had to start again under Alan Davies, and the first priority was to ensure that we made it hard for teams to score tries against us. We had been missing first-time tackles with a shocking regularity and the increasing pace of the international game meant that big scores were not the rarity of old, as Wales could well testify. As a young boy, I was well aware of the sense of shock when New Zealand defeated Wales 23–3 in 1980. By 1991, that would have been regarded as a triumph.

We finished joint second in the championship along with France and Scotland, having beaten the Scots 15–12 in Cardiff thanks to a try by flanker Richard Webster. He stormed over after a break by prop Hugh Williams-Jones that any outside half would have been pleased with, a jinking, feinting run that, he told us after-wards, covered some 50 yards. I had by then taken over from Colin Stephens at outside half, and if my defensive ability had leant itself to playing at inside centre, I preferred the greater involvement at half-back. It again worried me that a player had occupied the position for so short a time and had not been given a proper chance to prove himself even though the management had promised an end to the constant chopping and changing which had blighted Welsh selection policy for too long.

We had been well beaten by England, but Colin was never going to have a major influence on the game because we were up against it at forward. Once again a Wales outside half became a victim of the irrational, misguided and to me unfathomable belief that all Wales need is a darting, jinking number ten and all will be fine with the world. Colin was left permanently scarred by the experi-ence and he only won one more cap. He lost his confidence at Llanelli and ended up moving to Leeds, another waste. If rugby, or sport, for that matter, was purely about natural talent, I appreciate I would not have been so successful.

We only used 18 players in the championship. Alan stated at the outset that he believed in continuity and that players should be given the chance to prove themselves. An occupational hazard of being the Wales outside half, however, is that there is no settling-in period, and when you consider the players of international ability that Wales has had in the position in the past ten years, it is a travesty that so little has been seen of them. It is as well for the likes of Grant Fox, Michael Lynagh, Mark Ella, Joel Stransky and Andrew Mehrtens that they were not Welsh, because they would have struggled to have made a name for themselves.

And then there is Rob Andrew. He won 71 caps for England but would have been fortunate to have played 17 times for Wales, but then other countries have different expectation levels when it comes to outside halves. Within little more than a year, I was to be moved to the centre again. Temporarily. I had my trusted right boot but I also had a thicker skin than my rivals – and I needed it. Even though we had had a far better championship than anyone would have dared hope on our return from Australia, questions were still being asked in public.

It has always struck me during my time with Wales that when we win, praise is grudging, rarely fulsome. When we lose, it is like the roof caving in. It is a syndrome the England soccer and cricket teams have to endure, and I did not feel we received sufficient credit for 1992. It should have been better: we put France under periods of intense pressure without being able to breach their line, but at least we were in with a chance of beating them right up to the final whistle. The year before, in Paris, we had lost the game after just a few minutes.

The tone for our campaign was set in Paris. Tony Copsey, the Romford-born Llanelli second row who was so Welsh that he had a 'Made in England' tattoo indelibly stamped on his rear, very nearly made international rugby history in Dublin. Ten minutes into his début, he flattened his opposite number Neil Francis with a right-hander Mike Tyson would have been proud of. Tony made no attempt to disguise the punch: Francis had been indulging in a spot of shirt-grabbing and Tony let him have it.

The referee was England's Fred Howard, a no-nonsense official, and I thought Tony was going to go. Ieuan Evans, our captain, pleaded with Fred, pointing out that it was Tony's first cap, and he was let off with a warning. While there is no way I would advocate foul play, that aggression was what we needed that day. Copsey's punch sent a message to the Irish pack that although Wales may have been a soft touch for a few years, that was then and this was now.

Tony was fortunate to survive. He and I were to have a confrontation on an international field just a few months later, at the National Stadium. What should have been the biggest day of my career as a Pontypridd player turned out to be my lowest moment with the club. My face was to end up as red as my hair.

CHAPTER SEVEN

Dirt Gets under the Fingernails

You have to be prepared to get your hands dirty in modern rugby. The days when outside halves could regard tackling as an optional extra are long gone. It is a part of the game I enjoy and one of the reasons I considered turning to rugby league, even if my defence in the 1998 championship left something to be desired. Outside halves have an image of being pretty boys, above the rough and tumble of the forward exchanges, but I have always relished physical confrontation.

That is perhaps one reason why I have not only been moved about in my international career but why I have never been accepted in Wales as a true outside half. My predecessors included Jonathan Davies, Phil Bennett, Barry John, David Watkins, Cliff Morgan and Cliff Jones, silky runners who lived up to an image, even if there was a physical side to Jonathan with which he has rarely been credited. Rugby has moved on since then and an outside half who does not tackle is a liability. The Australian Mark Ella revolutionised the position. A superb passer and linker, he scored the majority of his tries supporting out wide. Very rarely would he try and break from first phase.

Outside halves are traditionally cool, calm and collected but I, perhaps because of the colour of my hair, am quick to anger and there are times when I have sailed close to the edge, too close on occasion, such as the 1992 Welsh Cup final between Pontypridd and Llanelli at the National Stadium. We knew we were up against it because Llanelli were then the supreme cup side, the masters of the competition.

We had hoped to draw Swansea, who were looking a little jaded after their league success, but we knew we were capable of reaching the final if we played at our best. My moment of madness ensured that the closest we got to the final was the television set, and instead of enjoying the summer playing and coaching in South Africa, I ended up feeling sorry for myself at home.

It all started when Llanelli called a Mark Ella move, the one which saw Ieuan Evans come into the midfield from the wing. I tackled Ieuan and Tony Copsey put his foot right on my chest. I grimaced in pain and saw red. We were 11–0 down and I had missed a couple of kicks, so I was not in the best of moods anyway. I kneed him. I was going to kick him but I held back. I only touched him gently, just to let him know what I thought of his footwork. The crowd started roaring and I ran back to my mark to get out of the way. The touch judge, Robert Davies, raised his flag and called over the referee, Derek Bevan. I knew they were not going to talk about the weather but I did not think it would be anything worse than a telling-off for me and a penalty to them.

Derek pointed at me and said, 'Come here, boy.' He looked at me in a reprimanding, headmasterly fashion and added, 'Kicking, off.' I said, 'You must be joking. That's ridiculous,' but he was not going to change his mind. I turned to apologise to my team-mates and trudged slowly off the field, unwrapping the strapping from my thumb for something to do. It was one of the most important days in the history of Pontypridd and I had blown it for them.

I sat in the changing-room with my head in my hands, disconsolate. I broke down. Cath came in along with Pontypridd's secretary Cenydd Thomas and they offered words of comfort, but all I wanted to do was go home. The players came in after the match, having lost but having performed heroically without me, and told me I was going out with them. We had an excellent reception at the club but the next day was a bad one. I knew that not only was I facing a six-week ban but, because it would stretch from one season to the next, it meant I could not play in South Africa in the summer.

I was being punished twice. It was not a six-week suspension but a five-month one. My contact in Eastern Province kept ringing to ask me what was happening but until I had the hearing before the WRU's disciplinary committee, which Pontypridd had asked for, there was nothing I could tell him. The Pontypool prop Lyndon Mustoe was due to fly out with me and he too was left in suspense.

The disciplinary hearing was a farce. Hearing was the right word for it, except that I listened and the WRU representatives spoke. I was accompanied by the Pontypridd president Sam Simon, a solicitor, but I was not allowed to call any witnesses or use video evidence to support my argument that I should not have been sent off. Nor could Sam help me in any practical way.

Our case hinged on a conversation between the touch judge and referee which had been heard by the television commentators. Derek was told that I had aimed a kick at Tony and that I had to be sent off. My mother was watching the match in the stand just behind Robert Davies and she had told me that, at the time, it looked as if I had gone in with my boot and that she was not surprised that I was ordered off. But video evidence showed clearly that I had gone in with my knee and virtually pulled out at the point of contact. Tony probably did not even feel it. He wrote a letter to the disciplinary committee saying that in his view I had not done anything to warrant a sending-off, but I doubt that a plea from the Pope would have made any difference. They had already made up their minds. I was asked for my version of events, but no video was watched in front of me.

I felt like a crook up before the magistrates. They sat three in a row, dispensing their version of justice. 'We have come to the conclusion that you will be banned for six weeks.' The irony was that I would not have been given a longer ban had I jumped up and down on Cops's head and forced him to spend a night in hospital. It seemed that no one was prepared to admit that a mistake had been made, and I was the one to suffer.

The sense of injustice I felt that day has not been dimmed by time. In retrospect, because I have spent every summer on tour since then, a few months at home did not do me any harm, but I was delighted when Mark Jones, the Ebbw Vale number eight, took the WRU to court in 1997 in protest at its antiquated disciplinary system. He won his case, and players who ask for hearings are now able to put their case properly, as I should have been allowed to.

I suppose Cops could afford to smile. Some six million people had seen him flatten Neil Francis with a belting punch which earned him no more than a warning, while I got five months for a tap. It highlighted the inconsistencies which bedevil the game, and since rugby went open in 1995 I have been an advocate of a third referee sitting behind a television screen to adjudicate on crucial incidents, such as a try or an act of foul play. In the 1997–98 Heineken Cup we lost two matches, against Bath and Brive, because tries were incorrectly awarded against us. The referee could not have been certain on either occasion, but we suffered. If the technology is there, why is the game afraid of using it? In case referees have to admit they were wrong?

If I was unfortunate then, I could not have complained had I been sent off at Twickenham in 1994. It was a game where both sides were chasing the championship, although because for the first time teams were going to be separated on points difference, England had to beat us by a pile to win the title – and they attacked us from the outset. We defended well that day and I put in 18 tackles, four behind flanker Mark Perego. I was marking Rob Andrew, a player I admired but one I enjoyed playing against because you invariably knew what he was going to do.

We had an altercation after he thought he was going to score a try. The whistle had gone for a knock-on but he carried on running, and as he went to pick the ball up he gave me a sly dig. I hit him across the head and flung my head at him. Luckily I did not connect, but the touch judge put his flag up and I thought I was going to be making another lonely walk.

Will Carling came running over, screaming, 'You head-butted him.' We had words before our wing, Nigel Walker, one of the nicest and most mild-mannered guys who has ever set foot on a rugby field, intervened and told Carling to get lost. I was lucky to get away with a dressing-down from the referee but Rob had the last laugh because he kicked the resulting penalty. It is an incident I do not look back on with any pride.

It was a mad championship for me because I had picked a dispute earlier in the year with the Ireland prop Peter Clohessy, an uncompromising character who is known as 'The Claw'. What came over me I do not know. We were playing at Lansdowne Road and something happened off the ball. I grabbed the first green shirt I saw, and unfortunately it belonged to Clohessy. 'Disappear, you fat slob,' I said to him, though less politely. He looked at me in disbelief. I repeated my request. 'I will have you for that,' he replied. I laughed and said in his dreams. I told him he would not come anywhere near me and to hurry on away. He ran off, shouting, 'I'll have you, I'll have you.' And he did.

You should never tempt fate. Clohessy was still seething with indignation when Ireland called a shortened line-out. Paddy Johns came on the charge and I tackled him. My father had always told me not to get caught at the bottom of a ruck, yet there I was when The Claw came chugging up. When he saw me a big grin broke across his face. He was as happy as a small boy clapping eyes on his Christmas sack. He jumped in and got me smack in the face. He laughed and ran off as I lay there, vowing never to take on a prop again.

I caught up with Clohessy when the Lions gathered for a training camp before we departed for South Africa in 1997. He reminded me about the incident and we had a laugh about it. He has had his share of strife with disciplinary committees, but in the few days I spent in his company he was an easy guy to get on with, and it was a big disappointment when he was forced to pull out of the Lions tour because of a back injury.

I have never felt in danger on a rugby field, although I have had my share of slipperings. Matches against French teams see you on your guard. When we played France in 1996, I had suffered a bad injury the week before. My eye was cut open at Abertillery and I needed 12 stitches in the wound. It was touch and go whether I would play against France, but as I had missed the three previous matches of the championship campaign there was no way I was sitting another afternoon out.

I took the field with the stitches still in the cut and I had a huge shiner. The game was only a couple of minutes old when I made a tackle and the French quickly piled in. Their hooker, Jean-Michel Gonzalez, came speeding in and, even though the ball had gone, shoved his fingers straight into the cut. He was giggling as he ran off to the other side of the field.

The French are adept at putting their knees into you and kicking lumps out of you. They are very sneaky and their speciality is the double knee in the back, which really hurts. They will do anything to get you out of the way and you have to stand up for yourself. I have had a few run-ins with Richard Dourthe, the Dax and France centre, a talented player but, as he has admitted, one whose head is in bits.

We played France in a midweek 'friendly', a word I use in the loosest sense of the term, in 1996. Dourthe and I bumped into each other. He said something uncomplimentary and than spat in my face before departing with a big grin. He was up to his antics later that season when Pontypridd played at Dax in the Heineken Cup.

We caught him out in midfield and Steele Lewis very nearly scored a try. He then ran up behind Stella and whacked him on the side of the head, felling him in an instant – and Stella takes some knocking over. Dourthe ran off with a look that said 'one-up', and we ended up losing the match, in my opinion because of weak refereeing. We had taken everything Dax had to offer, but the referee's decisions were all in their favour in the final quarter. The same thing was to happen to us the following year in Brive.

French crowds are intimidating. They are not used to seeing their side lose because of the nature of their club rugby, where everything is stacked against the away side. European rugby is different. Pontypridd are hard to beat at Sardis Road, but whenever we go away our attitude is that we are going to win. French clubs seem surprised by that and take offence if we do not roll over.

I have never got to know many French players well. The language barrier hardly helps, although after we had played them in 1992, Tony Clement and I sat outside the hotel where the post-match dinner was being held with Jean-Baptiste Lafond and Franck Mesnel, who both spoke fluent English. We had a few beers and decided that the dinner was not for us. Instead of sitting down to a five-course dinner dragged out over hours by a series of speeches, we ended up in Burger King, laughing and joking. The WRU was not amused, but dinners are arranged for committee men, not for players, and the time I spent in the company of Lafond and Mesnel was far more rewarding than being pinned down by a blazer who, having had too much to drink, is anxious to tell you what is wrong with your game.

I wish there were more interaction between players after matches, particularly now that the Heineken Cup has made its welcome introduction. But since rugby at the top has become professional, it seems to be going the way of soccer, which is a tribal sport. Money will mean an end to the innocence of old, but it does not mean that all the virtues of amateurism have to be abandoned.

What happened between Brive and Pontypridd in September 1997 was a source of particular regret. It wasn't so much what happened on the field – because rugby is a physical contact sport and flare-ups will often occur – but what happened off it afterwards in Le Bar Toulzac, and I fear that the ramifications of that will have a lasting impact.

Much is made in the media of what a dirty game rugby is, but if you listen to the players of yesteryear you realise it is cleaner now than it ever has been. No one would ever have been sent off in their day for a gentle tap with a knee. But they played in an era before the omnipresence of television cameras and touch judges programmed to flag. You can still get away with a few things, but the risk is enormous. Rugby may not yet be a game for angels, but perpetrators of dark deeds run a greater risk than ever before.

CHAPTER EIGHT

Chumps to Champs

If anyone had suggested at the end of 1991 that in little more than two years Wales would be the Five Nations champions, he or she would have had a job for life modelling strait-jackets. A year after our World Cup failure we came up against Australia, the champions, again at the National Stadium. Colin was back at outside half, having played in the friendly against Italy at the beginning of October when I was suspended. I had been chosen to play for Wales A against Australia ahead of Colin but was ruled out for a couple of weeks after damaging ankle ligaments at Swansea, and I missed the full international.

We did well against Australia. They won 23–6, David Campese scoring a last-minute try from 75 yards, his trademark in Cardiff, but they were made to fight all the way for the victory. It was clear that we had made significant progress under Alan, Bob and Gareth, and we went into the championship more confident than a Wales squad had been for years. Swansea and Llanelli had beaten the Wallabies and Welsh rugby was looking up.

Before the campaign started, we spent a week training in Lanzarote. The warm climate meant that we could get more work done outdoors, and the trip was good for bonding. The only problem was that the wheels came off at the end, literally, much to the disgust of the management.

We had decided to celebrate the end of a hard few days by having a couple of well-earned beers, and someone suggested it would be a good idea if we went for a mountain-bike ride. I am not sure how many of us would have passed a breathalyser test, but we piled on to the bikes and soon got involved in a pile-up. There was a big crash after a couple of the boys went too fast over a hill, and the prop Mike Griffiths ended up with a broken collarbone which put him out of the championship. A few others sustained cuts and bruises and Bob had more than a few words to say. A few journalists had spent the week with us enjoying a quiet time away from the office, but they were soon stirred away from the bar and into action when we crept back.

My room-mate in Lanzarote was Mark Perego, the Llanelli flanker, one of the hardest players I have ever come across. Pegs was an enigmatic figure, a loner who hated the social side of rugby. For him, rugby involved only training and playing. Supremely fit, he did not drink, and there were more than a few after-match dinners which Pegs attended in clothes borrowed from others which invariably did not match.

Everywhere he went he carried a porcelain pig with him which he called Mr Peeg, even putting it in his kit bag. He would turn up for team meetings and, as the coaches would point out the importance of this and that, Pegs would nod off. No one ever said anything because they knew that, when it mattered, on the pitch, he would get the job done.

He only played nine times for Wales because he would take unannounced breaks from the game. His last appearance was against Spain in the World Cup qualifier in Madrid in the summer of 1994. We had a tour of Canada and the South Seas immediately afterwards and Pegs was chosen. He pulled out for reasons the management did not accept and he was not considered again.

Pegs liked his own space and he would have been happy playing 20 years earlier, when rugby was a pastime and did not intrude so much on players' time. His nickname was Oddball, but I found him a straightforward guy. He knew his own mind and did things his way. As a player, he was exceptional. He got through an enormous amount of work on the pitch and he was the hardest tackler I have ever seen.

An attacker could have worked up a big head of steam, but if he ran into Pegs he would find himself in reverse gear. It is said that when Pegs won his first cap, against Scotland in 1990, as soon as the match was over he went for a run along the River Taff because he had not found the 80 minutes particularly tiring. He ended up drifting away from Llanelli to Leeds, but I do not think he will have any regrets about his career. He was not one to be dictated to and he shaped his own destiny. He was a top man and I was sorry when he disappeared from the scene.

When we returned from the warm of Lanzarote to the cold and wet of Wales, our thoughts turned to England, our first championship opponents. There were shades of 1991: they were the overwhelming favourites for the title and they had already beaten France at Twickenham in what was assumed to be the Five Nations decider. We were given no chance, having lost our previous three matches against them by significant margins.

We were up for it, however, and mentally sharp after Lanzarote where we had played a number of sports other than rugby to break up the routine: soccer, basketball, swimming and, of course, cycling. One of the downsides of professional rugby has been the monotony of training every day. Those players not fortunate enough to have sessions broken up become stale, and although they are physically in good shape, their minds are not right. As Pontypridd closed in on the league title in 1997, we often played soccer in training. It was therapeutic, and I believe that coaches at the leading clubs need to vary training to keep players mentally alert. Preparation is a vital part of the modern game, but since the start of professionalism, the extra time players have had has not been used that wisely in Wales.

The victory over England was one of the most satisfying moments of my international career. They had the majority of the play but they could not find a way through our defence, and a moment of typical opportunism from Ieuan Evans gave us the victory 10–9. Emyr Lewis, showing a delicateness and a precision not normally associated with back-row forwards, chipped into space from inside his own half, but England did not appear to be in any danger because Rory Underwood was yards ahead of Ieuan. Rory was strolling back without a care in the world when Ieuan came steaming up and hacked the ball on. By the time Rory had been shaken out of his slumber, Ieuan was diving on the ball over the line. I took the conversion from near the touchline and it went over to give us the lead. Even though there were still 40 minutes to play, there was no further scoring.

After the match, I could not understand why so many people were making a fuss about my conversion, saying it had won the match, when clearly Ieuan was the hero. When I took the kick I had assumed we were in front, and that took all the pressure off. It was only afterwards that I realised we had only won by a point. I had been so caught up in the atmosphere and the drama of the game that the scoreboard never registered.

The scenes after the final whistle were reminiscent of the good old days. The crowd swarmed on to the pitch and carried the players off shoulder-high. An abiding image is the picture of a smiling Gareth Llewellyn being held aloft by jubilant supporters, fists clenched in a victory salute. The win meant so much, not just to the players, but to the nation.

Because of Mike Griffiths's injury, the selectors had had to choose the uncapped Ricky Evans at prop, and hooker Nigel Meek was also making his international bow. Garin Jenkins had been banned for 16 weeks after being sent off playing for Swansea against Llanelli. Small wonder England hooker Brian Moore said before the match that there was no way he could see his side losing. Statements like that invariably come back to haunt you, though, as we were to find at Twickenham in 1998.

England had enough possession to win, but the beauty of the Five Nations is that it does not pay to take anything for granted. The relative failure of the three Celtic nations this decade has prompted some observers to suggest that the championship has no future, and that England and France should link up with Australia, South Africa and New Zealand and play a virtual World Cup every year. The Celts may still be coming to terms with the demands of the modern game, but the last thing professional rugby needs is a contraction at the top.

England and France should be working with Wales, Scotland and Ireland, not forgetting Italy, to ensure that the international scene in Europe is vibrant. By working together we can all help to ensure that a European nation has a chance of winning the World Cup in Cardiff in 1999, and that means playing each other regularly at all international levels as well as ensuring that the Heineken Cup becomes as important to our game as the Super 12 is to the three major southern hemisphere nations.

We should have had at least a share of the title in 1993 but, just as scoring an early try in an international sometimes leads to complacency, so we let the victory against England go to our heads. We went to Murrayfield two weeks later and our campaign started to go pear-shaped. We failed to muster a single point. A gale-force wind swirled around the ground, but Gavin Hastings had one of those days when everything he kicked went over.

We could not even tell who had the wind advantage when the game started and, looking back, we were over-confident. Scotland scored only one try, a dubious affair after all 16 forwards fell over the line together, but there was no questioning their superiority. We were brought down to earth and we had the consolation against Ireland of bidding to become the first Welsh team to win both their home matches in the championship for the first time in 12 years.

There is something about playing Ireland in Cardiff. We should have won but we lost 19–14 and I missed seven kicks at goal, one of my worst ever kicking displays. I was so drained of confidence in the second half that I asked Mike Rayer to have a go, but he told me to keep going. It was not to be, and yet the next day I went out and landed 20 kicks out of 20. To make matters worse, Eric Elwood, a newcomer to the Ireland side, landed his kicks and had an excellent all-round game.

I took the blame for the defeat, and rightly so, because my job was to put the kicks over and I failed abysmally. If my honeymoon had ended a while back, it was the start of an open season for attacks on me in the media, attacks which grew more strident, irrational and personal over the coming months. It was part of the territory as far as I was concerned, though. My only worry was that I had let the team down and I wanted to ensure that it never happened again.

I changed my kicking routine before matches. Up until then, I used to take 18 to 20 kicks on the Tuesday, Wednesday, Thursday and Friday before an international. I cut it down to six on a Wednesday and twelve on each of the next two days and I have not looked back, apart from the 1995 Welsh Cup final when I had the mother of all off-days with the boot against Swansea.

Wales finished the season bottom of the championship after losing to France in Paris. For the first time that season the selectors indulged in multiple changes, with six heads rolling after Ireland. I survived and put a kick over from the touchline. We scored our first try in Paris for ten years but were well beaten 26–10, and a campaign which had started on such a high turned out to be a massive anti-climax.

We knew we were a better team than our position showed and

we proved that in our next 13 matches. We lost only two, at home to Canada and away to England, and we won the championship in 1994, only the second time Wales had done so in 15 years. We had had a good tour of Zimbabwe and Namibia in the summer, with three comprehensive Test victories. I played at centre, full-back and outside half, and it was clear that Adrian Davies had become a serious challenger for my position.

I was back in the centre for the opening two matches of the 1993–94 season, against Japan and Canada in Cardiff. Ieuan scored a try from 50 yards after just 45 seconds in a comprehensive victory over the Japanese, but Canada pipped us. It was a night of personal triumph for me because I equalled the international record of eight penalties in a match, but that counted for nothing because we played badly against a committed but average side. Our forwards never got to grips with the Canadian eight but it was Adrian who took the rap for a defeat which stunned Wales, typically so for a nation which expects its outside halves to make silk out of a pig's ear of a job by the forwards. One of their tries came from a clearance kick by Adrian which was charged down, but we did not lose because of him.

The criticism changed him and I do not think he was ever the same player afterwards. I was back at outside half for the start of the championship against Scotland in Cardiff. It was only my 18th cap but it was already my fourth stint in the position. I had had enough of being moved around, and as I had been in good form for Pontypridd I intended to make the most of the opportunity. The fixtures fell perfectly for us that year because the games became progressively harder: Scotland were struggling, Ireland were hoping for big things after beating England the previous year, we had not beaten France anywhere for 12 years and our final opponents, England, were the dominant force in the championship.

The Scotland match started with a flurry of fists. Garin was blamed afterwards, but the Scots had decided to mix it at the start and we were in no mood to take any nonsense. Gavin Hastings missed a kick in front of the posts and we turned it on in the second half on our way to a 29–6 win. Mike Rayer came on as a replacement wing and scored two tries. We were on our way, but unlike the previous year there was to be no taking anything for granted.

Ireland were confident of beating us but Eric Elwood could not repeat his success of 1993 and, like Hastings, missed a vital kick in front of the posts. I scored all our points with a try and four penalties in our 17–15 win, but against France in Cardiff it was Scott Quinnell's day. He was awesome and put in as good an individual display as I have ever seen on an international field. He scored a try out of nothing from 40 yards, Frenchmen clinging on to him as he held the ball in one of his huge hands. He was the answer to our prayers, a huge presence at forward, but in less than a year he had joined the Welsh dynasty in rugby league. His performance in that match, however, was the stuff you can normally only dream of, and after the French had mounted a comeback he helped set up our decisive try, breaking through more tackles to send Nigel Walker, the former Olympic hurdler, speeding away on the left wing.

'The Flash' said goodnight to the French defence as it desperately tried to cover across in as quick a streak to the line as you will ever see. We had won three out of three and everything was going to be there for the taking at Twickenham: the Triple Crown, the Grand Slam and the championship. In less than three years, we had turned ourselves from laughing stocks into champions, an achievement for which I felt Alan, Gareth and Bob never received enough credit.

We never looked like winning at Twickenham, but heroic defending kept the score down to 15–8 and we could have sneaked a draw at the end when Scott was nearly through. We took the championship on points difference, the first time in the tournament's history that teams level on points had been separated, and although the immediate feeling after losing to England was one of disappointment, all the more so because Ireland had won there a month before, winning the title was a feat worth celebrating.

We had played the best rugby of the five nations. England, for all their virtues up front, only scored two tries in the four matches, both against us, and they showed little inspiration. We moved the ball well and we had the nucleus of a useful pack. The World Cup was little more than a year away and I was confident we had a squad capable of making at least the quarter-finals. It did not take long for the 1994 championship to become a distant memory.

CHAPTER NINE

Too Fly by Half

Ihave been dropped as the Wales outside half seven times in my career, sometimes from the team itself but more often moved to the centre or full-back. The road to glory is littered with the bones of those who were undone by the magic of the moment – and the pressure that the Welsh outside-half jersey brings with it. From the day you are first chosen in the position, you are made aware of your illustrious predecessors.

What no one bothers to say is that even David Watkins, Barry John and Phil Bennett were all dropped by Wales at some stage of their careers. Bennett returned home a conquering hero in 1974 after helping the Lions win their first series in South Africa. Less than a year later, Wales rated him their third best outside half behind John Bevan and Bernard Thomas. Barry John's first appearances for Wales were greeted with something less than rapture and Watkins regained his place.

What I have always found hard to understand is that, considering the pressures which come with the jersey, no attempt is made to help players adjust to the role. I have never spoken to Bennett or John about what it takes to come to terms with the expectation of being the Wales outside half, even though they are both high-profile media figures. I am fortunate in that, even though I have been dropped or moved to another position several times, I am still around to tell the tale.

Some of my contemporaries have not been so fortunate. I think in particular of Colin Stephens and Adrian Davies, two classical Welsh outside halves who, in terms of pure ability, probably had more to offer than me. The big advantage I had was my thick skin. I am a scrap merchant who does not care what people say about me. My objective has always been to do well for myself and for the team.

Some players believe what they read or hear and that infests them with self-doubt. Colin succeeded Jonathan Davies at Llanelli when he was only a teenager when he could have done with another couple of years sitting at the feet of the master, listening and learning. Jonathan is one of the greatest rugby players I have ever seen, but had he not turned professional at the beginning of 1989, he would possibly have lost his Wales place.

His last match was against Romania in Cardiff at the end of 1988. Wales lost and there was an outpouring of indignation. Jonathan was not only the Wales outside half but also the captain, and he bore the barrage of the criticism. He decided, understandably, that he had had enough of taking flak and cashed in on his ability. If there were some in Wales at the time who welcomed his departure, he left behind him a huge void which made people finally understand exactly how good he was.

Colin played four internationals in Wales in 1992, but he attracted a barrage of criticism, notably for his defence. It got to him and he lost his confidence. He failed to regain it at club level and he ended up leaving Llanelli for Leeds, a grievous loss to Welsh rugby. You could see his talent on the training field: his quick hands, his speed off the mark, his awareness and his huge boot. He was not the biggest guy around so he was going to be pushed to stop huge forwards on the charge, but he had more pure talent than some of the great outside halves in international history, Grant Fox, Michael Lynagh, Andrew Mehrtens, Naas Botha and Hugo Porta, to name but a few.

He had the misfortune to be playing at a time when Wales was not a rugby superpower, and he was a sensitive person. Talent is not everything in a player – temperament and judgement are other essential qualities – but there have been so many players like Colin in recent years, lost to the Welsh squad despite their ability, and the essential reason, to me, is that they have struggled to cope with the legacy of the past with no attempt made to help them.

Adrian Davies never recovered from our home defeat by Canada in 1993. Like Colin, he had a star-laden career as a schoolboy and he won four Blues with Cambridge University. He appeared to be born to play outside half for Wales. If Colin resembled Phil Bennett, Adrian brought to mind Barry John, with his shimmying running style, his ability to kick with either foot and his footballing ability. He was a natural.

He bore the brunt of the criticism for the Canada reverse and I moved back to outside half. Nothing was said about the fact that he had gone for 20 minutes in that match without receiving a pass. He had a kick charged down which led to a try, but he could not be held responsible for the defeat. We tried to take them on at forward and failed. That was not Adrian's fault, but when you are the Wales outside half you are judged not by how your pack plays but by whether or not you win the game.

I thought Adrian, a laid-back man, would have survived the criticism. He was a hugely influential player for Cardiff and his arrival coincided with the club picking itself up from the foot of the first division and becoming the strongest in Wales. I was amazed when Cardiff let him go to Richmond in 1996 because he was the player who made them tick. They had signed Jonathan from Warrington in a high-profile deal, but Jonathan was returning to a game which had changed considerably in the seven years he had been gone. By the time he learned what Adrian already knew, it was time for him to retire.

Adrian's international career was briefly resuscitated in the 1995 World Cup when his club coach, Alex Evans, took over from Alan Davies in a caretaker capacity, but he has not been involved in the Wales squad since. I thought, given his education, intelligence and cool demeanour off the field, that he would have coped with the load, but he never really had a run in the side and he never played in the championship. He has done well for Richmond, but as far as Wales is concerned it is a case of another one who got away.

I would like to sit down with Colin, Adrian, Arwel Thomas, Jonathan Davies, Barry John and Phil Bennett and talk about how it would be possible to help the Wales outside halves of the future. Arwel has been my main rival for the position since the beginning of 1996, but he has been in and out of the side, lauded one minute, written off the next.

The Wales outside-half jersey is gold among red, and the figure 10 is luminescent. You have to be mentally strong to keep hold of it. I have used criticism of me as a fertiliser, a source of nourishment. I know my weaknesses better than most, but I am also aware of my strengths. You have to be strong. You have to look after yourself because no one else will. When you are down, you find out who your friends are, but it is your family which feels the criticism the most. My mother and uncles get very upset, but I am like my father: let them all talk.

I have only twice responded to stick because I felt it had become personal. I saluted Brynmor Williams, who had not been recommending me for rugby's hall of fame, when he was in the radio box at Pontypool and I dropped a last-minute goal to win the match for Pontypridd, and, before the Scotland international in 1995, I pinned a newspaper article J.J. Williams had written on to the wardrobe door in my hotel bedroom. I was sharing a room with Robert Jones, my half-back partner, and J.J. had also made some derogatory comments about him. The gist of it was that neither of us should be playing for Wales because we could not run with the ball and were far too predictable. I am not sure that the article was written in the language J.J. would have used, but the sentiments were his and he had failed to address the way rugby had changed since his playing days in the 1970s. It is as well for Fox and Lynagh that they were not Welsh, because J.J. would have had them for not living up to an ideal. He wants Twinkletoes in an era when defences are more organised than ever before and when fitness programmes mean teams do not tire as they did in the 1970s when Wales used to make hay in the final 20 minutes of matches. Rob and I decided at Murrayfield in 1995 that we were going to show J.J., and Rob scored a cracking try in the opening minutes.

We both ran the ball and afterwards were criticised for not kicking more. It took a forward, the former Wales hooker Alan Phillips, to point out that if any other outside half had made the breaks I had, the response would have been positive. It was a question of image: I was not the sleek model which normally rolled off the conveyor belt of the Welsh outside-half factory, and to many I was never going to be acceptable. Rob and I went back to the hotel after the match, ripped J.J.'s article off the wardrobe and kicked it into the bin.

I do not mind what J.J. says but I hope he never runs into my mother. She is waiting to expel several years' frustration and anger, but I try to tell her there is no point in feeling that way. Only two players in the history of Welsh rugby have received more caps than me, I have been part of a winning Lions team in South Africa and I have won a cup and a league medal with Pontypridd. It does not matter what anyone thinks or says: I have not only achieved more than most other players, and far more than I dreamed was possible when I started my career, but there is, I hope, more still to come.

If I do not conform to everyone's ideal of an outside half, that is their problem. I would like my mother to see my career as a cause of celebration and not to get flustered by something that someone gets paid for saying. Your career is too short to hold grudges and become obsessed with whether or not the critics like you. As my career has progressed, I have become more like Scott Gibbs. I value my privacy and get away from rugby whenever I can. I have become more selective in my dealings with the media.

Whereas I used to say what I thought others would want me to say, I now tell it as I see it. I do not court the media and would be more than happy if I never gave another interview, but I am not concerned now about the opinions of others. It perhaps says something about the current state of Welsh rugby that I think the most perceptive commentator around is probably John Scott, the former England and Cardiff captain, who has a weekly column in the *South Wales Echo*.

Scott may have played in the 1970s and 1980s, but he does not live in the past. He writes as if he were still playing, and although he is not one to pull his punches, I appreciate where he is coming from. Perhaps because he is not Welsh, he is not tied down by a romantic notion of what the game should be about. He deals in reality and I respect his judgement. I just wish there were more like him, not for my sake but for the well-being of the game.

J.P.R. Williams had just stood down as an adviser to the Wales selectors in 1995 when an interview with him appeared in *The Observer*. He was quoted as saying – it was the year when we had been whitewashed in the championship and eliminated from the World Cup at the group stage – that many of Wales's problems stemmed from the lack of a fly-half. 'Neil Jenkins is a lovely lad who tackles and kicks so well. The Welsh don't want that. It is up to others to tackle. They want fly-halves to run and make beautiful, jinking breaks. We like nonconformists.'

A non-tackling outside half – more romantic twaddle. I

expected better of J.P.R., one of rugby's greats. When Wales won the Grand Slam in the year of my birth, their final match was in Paris. I have seen the match on video many times, and arguably the decisive moment in Wales's 9–5 victory had Barry John at the centre of it. Not the try he scored, or the penalty he kicked, but the tackle he made on France's huge number eight, Benoit Dauga.

John's frame was slender and he was not known for his hard tackling. He was happy to leave it to others, but when Dauga came charging at him he had no choice but to get in there. He received a broken nose, but he saved the try which, had it been converted, would have been worth five points to France, more than the difference between the sides at the end. I am not sure that J.P.R., who was then the last line of the Welsh defence, would have been too pleased then had John decided to step out of Dauga's way, and his comments in *The Observer* were unworthy of someone who had contributed so much to the game.

There is far more to outside-half play than making darting breaks. I am not blessed with the speed I had as a teenager and I look to make up for that lack of pace in other areas, such as taking the ball up, putting others into space, kicking and tackling, which, contrary to what J.P.R. believes, is an essential quality at outside half. Without it you have a weakness which sides ruthlessly exploit, as Colin Stephens found.

Grant Fox and Michael Lynagh were not defence-splitting outside halves, but their names are revered the world over. They were fortunate not to be born in Wales because they would have been roasted for not being jinkers and darters, but what players they were. They both had the advantage of playing behind strong packs, but they were both outside halves in the modern game who got their back-lines moving and who supported out wide, Lynagh especially. His try in the 1991 World Cup quarter-final against Ireland in Dublin was typical of the man.

There was less than a minute to go, Australia were trailing, and instead of going for the drop goal which would have sealed victory, he spread the ball in Ireland's twenty-two and popped up in the corner to take the scoring pass. Had he tried to jink his way through when he initially received the ball from a line-out he would have been swamped by green marauders, but Lynagh did not have to live up to an ideal and was judged simply on his own performances. And, like Fox, he could kick a goal or two.

When my Welsh career ends, someone else will be judged by the past. I hope they are strong enough to cope with it. I would like to be given the chance to talk to them, to tell them what to expect and how I coped with it. I cannot see myself as a coach when I retire, but I would not mind being a team manager in the mould of Robert Norster. He made a huge difference in the four years he was with Wales because he had an empathy with the players and you could go to him with a problem no matter how big or small.

Things do get on top of you and players need someone to turn to, but there is no one who can understand exactly what it means to be the Wales outside half unless you have pulled on the gold jersey. With it comes not just hope and hype; you are also expected to be the one who plucks Excalibur from the swirling river and rides to the rescue. Myths, fairy tales and legends.

CHAPTER TEN

Worlds Apart

Five Nations champions we may have been in 1994, but our poor display in the 1991 World Cup meant we had to take part in the qualifying round for the 1995 tournament in South Africa. The qualifiers were divided into two stages: a group section, the winner of which would be going to South Africa, followed by play-offs to determine which pool you would go into in the finals, and the one to avoid had South Africa and the holders Australia lurking in it.

Our first stop was Lisbon to face Portugal. Two months before it had been England at Twickenham for the championship, but we were quickly reminded of how far we had fallen at the beginning of the decade. I go into every match respecting the opposition, but there was never any doubt that we were going to defeat Portugal, a country without much of a player base. They scored a try but we ran in a few more and defeated them 102–11, an international record until Italy bettered it a few days later. I remember the match most for the unsuccessful attempts of the tannoy announcer to get his tongue around the Welsh pronunciations.

Three days later we took on Spain in Madrid. They were more organised and the scoreline of 54–0 flattered us slightly. The week away was like a training camp for our summer tour of Canada and the South Seas, which was to prove far more arduous. We avenged the defeat by Canada seven months previously in a superb team performance. They fancied their chances and had gone public with some uncomplimentary remarks about the incestuous nature of Welsh rugby, but we did our talking on the pitch and put them away 33–15.

We then had three Tests in a week in the South Seas. I was rested for the first, against Fiji, and Adrian Davies took over. I returned for the international against Tonga, when I teamed up with my half-back partner at Pontypridd, Paul John, for the first time in a full international. I kicked all the points in our 18–9 victory, but Western Samoa in Apia three days later proved a match too far.

The temperature in the shade was 98 degrees. I had never played in heat like it and, together with the fact that we had played five internationals in the previous five weeks, it meant we did not have the legs to cope with the rampant Samoans. Their number eight Pat Lam scored a try after a chip and chase which we did not have the energy to follow. We had changed in a tent whereas they had air-conditioned accommodation, and after the match our scrum half Rupert Moon collapsed with heat exhaustion. We had expected the worst after seeing locals arrive for the game armed with umbrellas.

It was hot when we played our next international, against Romania in Bucharest that September. We had to win and then defeat Italy in Cardiff the following month to ensure that we were in the same group as New Zealand and Ireland in the World Cup. We had heard various tales about the perils of visiting Romania as far as hotels and food were concerned, and the abiding impression you were left with was the poverty in the city, battered cars competing with horses and carts for space on the road and buildings decaying, reminders of an opulent past.

Our hotel was excellent, however, and food was in plentiful supply because there was a major tennis tournament going on at the same time. We played in the football stadium in Bucharest, a huge arena with a 100,000 capacity. The match was not quite a sell-out, 3,000 spectators managing to squeeze in. I was struggling with shin splints and was in pain throughout the whole match. Romania took a grip at forward but we won thanks to a moment of inspiration from Ieuan Evans, who scored a try out of nothing. It turned out to be a ten-point try because I converted it and then landed the penalty from halfway which had been awarded because a defender had kneed Ieuan in the back after he had scored.

We eased home 16–9 but were pushed all the way by Italy at the National Stadium. I kicked 24 points in our 29–19 success, which took me past Paul Thorburn's total of 304 points for Wales. What was more important was that we had booked our place in the same group as Ireland. With the top two teams going through, it was a question of who was going to accompany the All Blacks into the quarter-finals. We fancied our chances against Ireland. Romania were locked with Australia and South Africa, while Italy had the pleasure of England, Argentina and Western Samoa. We had given ourselves every chance of making up for 1991.

Our next international, against South Africa in Cardiff, gave us further cause for hope. We lost 20–12 to the team which was to win the World Cup and we had secured enough possession to win, had we had a shade more self-belief and run the ball at them. It augured well for the defence of our Five Nations title, but within four months we were in a state of disarray and the careful rebuilding which had taken place since the summer of 1991 turned to rubble in a wanton act of vandalism.

Whereas in 1994 our championship programme had been neatly structured so that the matches became progressively harder, our first match in 1995 saw us visit Paris, and we duly lost 21–9. We had already been hit by injuries, with Mike Rayer, Ieuan Evans and Nigel Davies all absent, and the prop Ricky Evans was not to last the match. He was taken to hospital for an X-ray on his leg, an injury we assumed had been caused in an accidental fall.

We discovered later that he had been head-butted by the France second row Olivier Merle and that he had broken his leg as he fell to the ground. It was too late for the Wales management to cite Merle, who was eventually dropped for one match by his coach Pierre Berbizier. The French Union said that the incident had bordered on dangerous play and that there was no relation between the butt and Ricky's injury, a piece of verbal dexterity which left us flummoxed. True, Merle did not plant his head on Ricky's leg, but it followed that if the lock had not decided to indulge in thuggery, Ricky's season would not have been at an end.

Merle decided to launch an astonishing defence of his action as he looked ahead to the match against England the following week. 'England will have to find something other than newspaper hacks to prepare their team. The Five Nations Championship is not there to perpetuate the One Hundred Years' War. As for the black-smith's brute, which I have been called, the English continue to utilise their press in order to wind things up. Thankfully, I know that the French press is intelligent.' Thankfully so was Berbizier: Merle watched the action at Twickenham on his television set, having virtually ended Ricky's career.

We were unable to repeat our 1993 performance against a street-wise England and again failed to score a try, losing 23–9. Prop John Davies was sent off and banned for 60 days for an alleged stamp on England flanker Ben Clarke. The referee was a Frenchman, Didier Méné, and as John reflected on his punishment, you could not help wondering about the injustice of it all. Merle was defended by his Union for a blatant act of violence and then one of its referees sends a player off for something which the television replay showed was nowhere near as cynical, dangerous or career-threatening as Merle's butt. The wheels of justice, and progress, turn so slowly in rugby union that incidents are not judged on their merits but on protocol.

Two down with two to go, we thought we would be able to salvage our season against Scotland and Ireland. Despite the advantage of Robert Jones's early try at Murrayfield, the Scots gained their revenge for their heavy defeat in Cardiff the year before. They were lying in wait for us and bombarded our line. Gavin Hastings had one of his better days with the boot. I had made one or two remarks to him the previous year when he was struggling at the National Stadium. 'Like that one, did you, boyo? Good, wasn't it?' he said to me as another kick sailed over. There was nothing I could say in reply because we were outplayed, and we had to salvage our self-respect against Ireland.

It was an important match at the National Stadium, not just because the loser would end up with the wooden spoon and the whitewash but because victory would provide a psychological edge before the World Cup. We were edged out in a dreadful match and for the third time in four games we failed to score a try. Ieuan Evans and Nigel Davies were back from injury, but we played without any confidence or fluency, a pale shadow of the champions we had been.

'A neutral observer might have felt like asking for his money back,' said the Ireland coach Gerry Murphy. The 80 minutes hardly led to a flurry of inquiries about the availability of tickets for our World Cup meeting with Ireland at Ellis Park that June, but it was typical of an international between Wales and Ireland, with the home side struggling to take the initiative. We still felt we would have the beating of them in South Africa.

Unfortunately, as so often happens in Wales, the politicians stepped in. No sooner had the first course been served in the after-match dinner than word was going round that J.P.R. Williams had resigned as an adviser to the national selectors, a role that was not clearly defined anyway, and that Geoff Evans, a selector, was considering his position. They were unhappy that decisions taken at a selection meeting were allegedly overturned by the Wales management.

'There is no point in having a selection panel if they are going to be overruled by the coach,' said Williams. I would have thought the coach's voice would have been paramount. After all, it was his neck on the block, and if he wanted someone, or was against the inclusion of someone else, that should have been the end of the story. It seemed to me that there was a bigger agenda to all this: Alan Davies, while popular with the players, did not have many supporters on the WRU's general committee. Our poor champion-ship campaign and Williams's resignation had given fuel to those who had been waiting to invite Davies to walk the plank, but I did not think that, just two months away from the World Cup, the Union would sack the coach.

It never pays to underestimate the capacity of Welsh rugby for self-destruction. Within nine days of the Ireland defeat, Alan Davies, Robert Norster and Gareth Jenkins had, according to reports, handed in their resignations. They had asked the Union if it wanted them to stay on. Not receiving an answer in the affirmative, they said their farewells. They were shown the door and they went through it with dignity. They were not thanked publicly for their efforts, which was churlish and ungracious of the WRU.

There could be no disputing that the three had presided over a period of relative success, but the Union had forgotten where Wales had come from under Davies, Jenkins and Norster. The laughter we had roused in 1991 had died in time. The pathetic spectacle that we had made of ourselves on and off the field in those dark days had given way to something far more respectable. The three seemed to have been judged on 1994 rather than three years earlier, and the WRU committed suicide as far as the World Cup was concerned.

The Union appointed a three-man coaching panel to take

charge for the World Cup: Alex Evans of Cardiff, Swansea's Mike Ruddock and Dennis John. Along with Gareth Jenkins they were the most successful coaches in Welsh rugby, but despite all their qualities they did not combine effectively as one. Alex was in overall charge, and Dennis and Mike did not lend themselves naturally to a subordinate role. The result was a build-up of tension within the squad which surfaced before the crucial Ireland match. Alan Davies departed, so we were told, to enhance our chances of making the quarter-finals of the World Cup; in reality his absence made sure we did not.

Which is to take nothing away from Alex Evans. I enjoyed his training sessions. He was a coach of proven pedigree, having been the Australian number two in the 1980s, and he had made a significant impact with Cardiff. He was a no-nonsense Aussie who lived and breathed rugby. It could have been argued that it had become a little too cosy in the Wales fostered by Alan Davies, with some players perhaps taking their places for granted, but there was no complacency with Alex around. He would bawl out slackers in training and he was quick to anger if mistakes were made, such as dropped passes or poor restarts.

I welcomed that, but he had no time to impose his own pattern and beliefs on the squad. The World Cup squad showed a number of changes from the players the previous management would have taken. There was no Phil Davies or Nigel Davies, good friends of mine, and no Paul John. Ieuan Evans was replaced as captain by Mike Hall, Alex's skipper at Cardiff. The two were on the same wavelength and I could see the logic of the decision, but all it did was reinforce the supremacy of Cardiff, a recipe for disunity on the scale of 1991 when Neath were to the fore.

Ieuan was respected throughout the rugby world as a player and as a leader. It was the second mistake of our World Cup campaign. There is no question that Mike Hall was worth his place in the team – he was a powerful, uncompromising centre – but he had no time to earn the respect of the other players or gain their full support. If the decision was unjust on Ieuan, it was also unfair on Mike – but who is going to turn down the chance of captaining their country?

The campaign remained on track for the first two matches, against Japan and New Zealand, but the test was going to be the first decision made by the three coaches: the team to face Ireland, the last and most important match of the three. Up until that selection day, there had been a superficial unity. We defeated Japan comfortably, with the wing Gareth Thomas scoring three tries on his international début. I played in the centre outside Adrian Davies, but he injured his ankle and I was back at outside half for the midweek clash against New Zealand.

We had a coach feeling his way, a captain who was fresh to the experience, and we also had a new manager, Geoff Evans, a second row with London Welsh, Wales and the Lions in the 1970s. He was no Robert Norster – not surprisingly, because he belonged to a different generation – and so he never started to fill the role Norster had played so successfully. Evans's major contribution to the campaign was to rile the All Blacks.

Addressing a press conference called to announce the Wales team, Evans stunned the assembled journalists by saying that Wales were bigger, stronger and fitter than the All Blacks. I am all for being positive before a match, but not to the point where you belittle your opponents, especially ones who have been vastly superior to you for a number of years. Even the Wales of Geoff Evans's day failed to beat New Zealand. To compound the error, Evans had the All Blacks thrown off Ellis Park after they had turned up for a light run-out the day before the match.

Geoff Evans ensured New Zealand were fired up. In the event, we contained them reasonably well without ever being in a position to win the match. We conceded fewer points against them than Ireland had and Scotland and England were to, but they were better and fitter than us. We defended strongly, apart from gifting them two of their three tries, and after one of their scores, their captain and hooker Sean Fitzpatrick ran past me and said, 'What do you think of the All Blacks, mate? Awesome, aren't we?' I was not going to argue with him, but Fitzpatrick and his forwards, in their desire to prove Geoff Evans wrong, slightly lost sight of their gameplan, and they were less expansive against us than against any other team in the tournament. With Jonah Lomu lurking on the wing, that was just as well.

The following day, the team to play Ireland was chosen. It was the moment of reckoning. The players were all gathered in the team-room, waiting to be summoned upstairs to see Mike and Dennis to be told the good, or the bad, news. It was like being back at school. Alex was not around. He should have been because, ultimately, the team was his. You knew who was in the side because they returned downstairs smiling. Those who had been left out disappeared to their rooms for a few moments of contemplation. I was not invited for a chat because Adrian Davies had told me he was at outside half and that I was in the centre with Mike Hall.

The main chance of keeping our World Cup campaign alive, ensuring that the squad was united, was lost. If it was not 1991 revisited, some of the players who were left out were unable to mask their disappointment. The repair work of the Alan Davies years had been unravelled in almost an instant, and it was just as well that Wales were hosting the 1999 World Cup finals – because it meant we did not have to pre-qualify.

CHAPTER ELEVEN

Heartbreak Hotel

The first mistake we made against Ireland was to receive the kick-off. Restarts have been a weakness in the Wales team for longer than I care to remember. We should have started the match by burying the ball deep in Irish territory, but instead we allowed them to put the pressure on us and before we knew it we were two tries down and chasing the game. There was so much at stake, but we started with a whimper.

We pulled back to one point by the end, but we had left our comeback too late. Ireland's third try was given despite a blatant knock-on by Eddie Halvey, but overall we could have no complaints. We had known that Ireland would start with a furious energy which would burn itself out. We had to contain them and hit them as they tired. We succeeded with the second, but failed miserably with the first.

We were ready for them. The preparations went well and we were focused when we ran out, but we let them come at us and gifted them two soft tries. It was another low point in my career, and instead of preparing to face France in the quarter-finals in the warmth of Durban, we found ourselves in a chilly hotel close to Johannesburg Airport, waiting to be given a flight home. We were there for a couple of days and we dubbed it 'Heartbreak Hotel', because all the teams who had been knocked out at the group stage were there: the Ivory Coast, Romania, Japan, Tonga, Argentina, Italy, Canada and Wales. It showed how far we had fallen. The revival in 1994 had been nothing more than a blip. There were no debriefings afterwards with the management; there was nothing to say.

We had spent four years building up to the World Cup and it was all for nothing. In the months after we returned home, there were various stories about how indisciplined the squad had been, with players going out drinking until the early hours of the morning. Alex Evans, in particular, had strong words to say.

There is no doubt that some players lost heart after the team to face Ireland was chosen, but there was no repeat of Australia 1991. Alex's main problem, like Ron Waldron's four years before, was that he was closely identified with one club, and there were a number of Cardiff players in the squad who, it could be argued, were there primarily because of the club they played for. It does not matter whether the argument has any validity: it did contribute to a lowering of the morale that had been built up under Alan Davies.

I do not blame Alex. Like Ron, he wanted to be surrounded by those whom he trusted, players who knew what he was about. Cardiff were one of the strongest clubs in Wales, if not Britain, but we had found out before that success at club level is not a reliable barometer for the international scene. It just raised the question of what the WRU expected when it got rid of the Alan Davies regime.

The idea of putting the top three coaches in Welsh club rugby together was always going to be fraught with danger. A number of egos landed in the same basket and the result was a scramble. All three were capable of coaching Wales in their own right, but together they made an uneasy alliance. Alex's training methods were interesting and varied, and had he had enough time I am sure we would have done better against Ireland, but it was not the players or the coaches who bore the prime responsibility for what happened in South Africa. The WRU had the most to answer for.

It was hard watching the rest of the tournament on television after returning home. All the talk was about Jonah Lomu, the 20-stone New Zealand wing who had taken the World Cup by storm. We had managed to stop him scoring a try and it was interesting that the All Blacks had switched him to the right wing against us, even though he is left-handed and left-footed. Ieuan Evans was mightily relieved. He had had to mark Va'aiga Tuigamala during the Lions' 1993 tour of New Zealand and still bore the scars of trying to stop a runaway tank.

Lomu was even bigger and quicker. 'Freak' was the word most

often used to describe him, because he embodied two of the qualities needed by top rugby players: power and pace. Most mortals have one or the other, but Lomu had both, and the fields he played on were littered with the bodies of defenders who had tried to fathom out a way of stopping him, without success.

Any major sporting tournament needs a personality like Lomu, because it takes a game beyond its natural boundaries. Millions all over the world who might not have had a close interest in rugby union would have been well aware of Jonah Lomu by the end of the World Cup. He was getting all sorts of offers, being asked to advertise this or that and being made a lucrative offer by the gridiron team Washington Redskins. His manager is a Welshman, Phil Kingsley Jones, and I mean no disrespect when I say that I wish their nationalities had been reversed.

New Zealand were by some way the best team in the 1995 World Cup. The way they demolished England in the first quarter of their semi-final in Cape Town was awesome. The All Blacks created the impression of being a free-running side, but they were deliberate and calculating, kicking when they had to and running when something was on. They surprised England by seeking width rather than contact early on and Lomu had used three players as a doormat within the first ten minutes. Game over.

To think that Geoff Evans had said Wales were bigger, stronger and fitter than the All Blacks . . . It was not a mistake Bob Norster would have made. After seeing England get hammered, I realised we had not done badly to keep their score down to 34, but they were singing from a different song-sheet from us. I thought they would win the final, even though South Africa had home advantage and strong emotional support to encourage them to mark the end of the post-apartheid era with a victory which would unite a nation which had been badly divided.

South Africa were fortunate to make the final because I felt France outplayed them in the semi-final in torrential rain in Durban. South Africa's try looked dubious and France were denied a similar effort, but the Springboks seemed destined to win the World Cup. They were an efficient, well-organised team whose tactics in the final were clear: to prevent Lomu from doing any damage.

The All Blacks played at half-pace because several of their players had gone down with food poisoning the night before and had been kept awake by the sound of car alarms going off outside their hotel in the early hours of the morning. Dirty tricks were suspected, but New Zealand were undone by a strong defensive operation and South Africa just about deserved their extra-time victory.

The Springboks milked the applause, so it was ironic two years later when they criticised the Lions after we had won the series there. We were, said a number of South Africans, a defensive team which relied on kicks rather than tries and had little sense of adventure. Yet we played as South Africa had in that World Cup final, and the tactics were applauded then. No one minded how the World Cup was won, only that the Webb Ellis trophy had come to South Africa at the first time of asking. Their reaction in 1997 only showed what bad losers they were, and it made our success all the more sweet.

New Zealand were to gain a measure of revenge the following year when, for the first time, they won a series in South Africa, but as the 1999 finals loom nearer, it may be that the All Blacks have already reached their peak. They have lost key players in Sean Fitzpatrick and Zinzan Brooke, and South Africa have emerged from a lean spell. The Lions played them at exactly the right time.

I next caught up with Lomu, figuratively speaking, at the end of 1995 when he played in Ieuan Evans's testimonial match in Llanelli. His success had not made him arrogant, despite a media intrusion most players never have to experience. He was a young man, just 20, who had had to grow up very quickly and a rugby player who inspired a mixture of fear and admiration in opponents, but off the field he was quiet and unassuming.

He was happy to pay tribute to Ieuan, whom he recognised as one of the world's leading players in his position. Lomu is a humble man who is excellent company off the pitch. I was unable to play in the testimonial match because Pontypridd had an important game a few days later, but I persuaded Gareth Jenkins to let me on for the last five minutes.

The players who turned up showed the regard in which Ieuan was held: Lomu, Sean Fitzpatrick, Jason Little and Gavin Hastings were among several big names. Every time Lomu had the ball a shoal of defenders pounced on him, hanging on to anything in a desperate bid to bring him down. The spectators loved it, and his presence helped to ensure a deserved capacity crowd for Ieuan.

Lomu came over with Phil Kingsley Jones and stayed in Phil's home village of Blaina in Gwent. While out for a quiet drink one night, Jonah was hit by violent toothache and had to pay an emergency visit to the dentist. The tooth had to come out and the poor dentist was to tug for about an hour to remove the offending molar which, he said afterwards, was more like a tusk than a tooth. Another chapter was added to the legend of Jonah Lomu.

Wales had found themselves back in South Africa just two months after returning home from the World Cup with their heads hung low. The WRU, in its wisdom, had decided it would be a good idea to start the season with an international in Johannesburg to mark an anniversary of one of the South African Union's sponsors. It was an extraordinary decision, irrespective of the fact that South Africa were on a high after winning the World Cup.

Our warm-up match was against South-Eastern Transvaal. Alex Evans remained in charge as caretaker coach, although this was to be his last international. We were without a number of players who had appeared in the World Cup and I was back at outside half. The team against South-Eastern Transvaal contained only one player who had played against Ireland. We were routed 47–6 in a dreadful performance against modest opposition. They were well into their season, while ours had not started and our rustiness was only too apparent.

I was on the bench but came on at full-back after 30 minutes when Justin Thomas was injured. I was soon contemplating an up-and-under and their number eight flattened me and put in a cracking punch. I vowed that I would go back there with a stronger side and exact revenge. I had to wait less than two years, and I was at outside half when the Lions played Mpumalanga, as South-Eastern Transvaal had become. We put 64 points on them and, right at the end of the match, I tackled the number eight and planted my elbow in his face. 'Who's laughing now?' I asked him. He said something in Afrikaans but, as I had found out to my cost before, what goes around comes around.

Wales were better in the Test match, which was played at Ellis Park in Johannesburg, the ground where our World Cup ambitions had perished. It was the first international played after the decision of the International Rugby Board the previous month to end amateurism, and the South African Union had wasted no time in putting some of their players on contracts said to be worth £140,000 a year.

Their second row, Kobus Wiese, paid some of his wages back immediately. We started the Test strongly and took the lead with a try by flanker Mark Bennett. As we celebrated the score, Wiese sneaked up behind our giant second row Derwyn Jones and floored him with a punch from behind. None of the officials saw the blow, but it was obvious something had happened because Derwyn was lying spark out on the ground.

He had to be helped from the pitch and replaced just four minutes into the match. We knew that the Springboks had been worried that, at 6ft 10ins, Derwyn would dominate the line-out, but Wiese wasted no time in sorting out the problem. Ellis Park had a Jumbotron which replayed significant moments to the crowd but, strangely, they did not enjoy the privilege of seeing our score again, a mistake which was rectified in the second half when Garin Jenkins, our hooker who had come on as a replacement flanker, indulged in a drop of the hard stuff.

Wiese did not get away with his particular brand of justice because the Wales management cited him. He was banned for 30 days and relieved of £9,000. Garin also got 30 days for punching scrum half Joost van der Westhuizen, but instead of being asked to part with cash he received some. As he walked off the field, the crowd pelted him with coins and oranges, egged on by continued replays of the incident on the big screen which, I believe, prompted the referee to order him off.

We had lost the game by then, but going into the last quarter we were only trailing 18–11. Had Wiese been sent off – and he should have gone – we would have been in with a chance. Even though we fielded a young side, with five players products of the previous season's Under-21 squad, we got stuck in and asked a few questions of them. At the end of the day, 40–11 was another record defeat, but we did enough to show that we should have made the quarter-finals of the World Cup. The match marked another milestone for me because I passed 400 points in international rugby, having stood on 399 after the Ireland débâcle.

At the end of the short tour, it was clear that the new world of professionalism was not going to help bridge the gap which had opened up between Wales and the major nations in the south. While members of the South African squad were negotiating large six-figure contracts, we were told by our Union that, as there was not much money in the kitty, Test players could look forward to an annual sum of around £20,000. Don't give up the day job, boys. I was fortunate because I had superb employers in Just Rentals, but most players faced a dilemma: did they take a chance and give up their jobs to become full-time rugby players, not knowing whether it would be worth their while financially, or did they carry on working and meeting their rugby commitments in their spare time?

It was not long before we were to be introduced to Wales's first full-time national coach. Alex Evans relinquished his caretaker role when we returned to Wales and went back to Cardiff, although it was not long before he went back home to Australia after being appointed coaching organiser of the ARU. Alex had not had much time to get his ideas across, but he was clearly a coach of pedigree, and in the right circumstances I am sure he would have made an impact. He may have been an Aussie, but his love and knowledge of the game were only too apparent. I learned a lot from him, but by the time we played Fiji in November, Kevin Bowring, who had graduated from the Wales Under-21s and Wales A, was in charge.

He was totally different from Alex. His approach to the game was more intellectual, whereas Alex had looked to motivate players and was very good one-on-one. Alex was a strong believer in establishing supremacy up front, the Australian way, something it was always going to be difficult for Wales to achieve because we lacked the height and bulk of countries like South Africa and Australia. Kevin was more keen for us to play in the traditional Welsh way, relying on cunning and guile rather than force – but you still had to win enough ball. And therein lay the rub.

CHAPTER TWELVE

Different League

The moment I had anticipated ever since I started playing first-class rugby arrived a few weeks after our ignominious end in the 1995 World Cup. Sheffield Eagles made me a firm offer to turn professional and I had a look around the club with my fiancée, Cath. I had had several approaches before, notably from Warrington, Widnes and Bradford Northern, but this was the first time a detailed contract had been put in front of me.

It was tempting, very tempting. Welsh rugby had slipped back into a state of despair after it had appeared we had learned from the dark days and recovered our credibility. It was clear from our time in South Africa that rugby union was not going to hold on to its cherished amateur status for much longer.

The three major southern hemisphere nations had clinched a television deal with Rupert Murdoch which would allow them to put their leading players on full-time contracts. The money was timely, because a former Australia player, Ross Turnbull, was trying to sign players up to a professional circus. Team hotels were ablaze with rumour and the intrigue continued after the tournament.

Turnbull was said to be being bankrolled by Murdoch's rival media magnate in Australia, Kerry Packer, and he was looking to sign up national squads. He came close to succeeding, and may well have done so had not the International Rugby Board announced that August that rugby union was to become an open game. Money was no longer a dirty word.

The Board has since been criticised for rushing into professionalism, but it had little choice because a number of players had pledged themselves to Turnbull. The transition from amateurism to professionalism was achieved smoothly in the south – not least because they had for a long time found ways to get round the strict regulations regarding material rewards – but in Europe it was not long before clubs and unions were at each other's throats.

It made for an unedifying spectacle. Professionalism ensured that the game in Britain, especially England, achieved a higher profile, but most of the media attention was given over to a civil war waging between the unions and the clubs, many of whom in England had been taken over by millionaire businessmen who wanted to see a return on their considerable investments.

The year which followed the Lions' tour of South Africa was the most disappointing of my career. It was not just that I had come down from a high after our series victory, but that the Welsh club game was being torn apart. Precious few league games, shrinking crowds and daily stories in the newspapers about renewed strife between the leading sides and the Welsh Rugby Union all contributed to a feeling of unease which, in part, contributed to heavy defeats against England and France in the Five Nations.

I had always fancied playing rugby league. The physical nature of the game, far from deterring me, appealed. I have always been one of the most prolific tacklers in the Wales team, and whereas in the past there have been some Welsh backs who have failed to make it up north because of the increased defensive work they suddenly find they have to do, I was confident I would make the adjustment.

I had followed rugby league since I was a boy, travelling regularly to see Wigan, and I went to a number of Challenge Trophy finals with my father. Wales used to have a fear of rugby league which bordered on the irrational, primarily because of the number of players who had been lured to the game. Because rugby union in Wales has always been essentially a working-class game, unlike its traditional middle-class standing in England, Ireland and Scotland, we have always been susceptible to raids by league clubs.

Money was never the main attraction for me, although when my father's company went bust and I had to look for a living elsewhere, the prospect of being paid to play rugby did interest me. League was simply a game I wanted to play. I have never been one of those who is for one of the rugby codes and against the other. They may be played with the same-shaped ball, but that is all they have in common. They are as different from one another as they are from the other codes of football, association and American.

I always wanted Wigan to come in for me and I would have signed for them without a moment's hesitation. There were rumours, but there was never any official approach. Rugby league clubs often contact you through intermediaries or scouts: 'Would you be interested in a move?' Your name would be passed on if you said yes, and it was then up to the club you had been recommended to to make the next move.

I only had two serious approaches. The first was from Warrington in 1991 after Wales's tour of Australia. It did not amount to a formal contract, but I was not ready to switch codes then – even though my father, who, like me, was a rugby league follower, urged me to sign. His reasoning was that if I turned down the chance it might never materialise again, and I could suffer a career-ending injury which would leave me with nothing. I preferred to bide my time.

I was far closer to signing for Sheffield. My father's advice was again to go for it, and my family, my parents and my future in-laws, accompanied Cath and me to Sheffield. The first thing which struck me was how far Sheffield was from Wigan and how long it would take to get there from Wales. The Sheffield Eagles were a new club anxious to make an impression and we were invited to watch them at Halifax. It was not the choicest of venues – a ramshackle ground fitting the cloth-cap image league was trying to shake off – and I think they guessed that night what my answer would be.

I was tempted because at the age of 24 I had played in a World Cup and achieved everything in union that I had hoped to – apart from being chosen by the Lions. I was also concerned about the future for Wales and Welsh rugby: we had taken a couple of steps backwards in 1995 and I did not know who the new national coach was going to be. I was caught in two minds and it was Cath who made the decision. She did not fancy settling down in Sheffield and, to the disbelief of my father, I decided to stay where I was.

I still thought I would end up a rugby league player, but within a few months the WRU contracted its leading players and clubs were allowed to pay. Together with my job with Just Rentals, it meant that rugby league was not going to provide me with a financial incentive to move. It was a case of Wigan or nothing, and the telephone never rang.

I do not see many Welsh players making the move north in the future because most of those who did so in the past only did so for the money and the security it offered. With English rugby union clubs offering generous contracts, players now have the opportunity of boosting their bank balances without having to learn a new game. Some of the players who have returned from league may decide to go back one day, and there is always talk in South Wales of a club being set up to be fast-tracked into the Super League, but the days of the mass exodus are over.

The bigger threat to Welsh rugby today comes from English union clubs. I was given permission by Pontypridd to speak to Bath during the 1997–98 season and other Allied Dunbar Premiership sides made it known that they would be interested in signing me. My profile had risen during the Lions tour, but I had never considered leaving Pontypridd unless it was to become a rugby league player. When I had been out of work at the beginning of 1992, Llanelli and Swansea had promised me jobs if I signed for them. I was only a couple of days away from joining Llanelli before Pontypridd secured me an interview with Just Rentals. As rugby union was an amateur sport then – at least in the sense that you were not able to earn your living playing it – a job was a major card into tempting a player to move clubs, especially one which allowed him to devote time to training and playing without any fear of recriminations. Just Rentals have proved the perfect employers for me and they, together with the community spirit fostered by Pontypridd, have combined to suppress my wanderlust. The attraction of Bath's offer was not financial; it was made shortly after Pontypridd had been due to face Cardiff in the league at the Arms Park, a fixture which degenerated into a farce without a ball being kicked, and it seemed to sum up the state of Welsh rugby.

Cardiff had long been in dispute with the WRU. It centred on the club's refusal to sign a ten-year agreement to remain locked into the Union in return for an annual income from money generated by the competitions they played in. The root of the problem was that Cardiff, the one club in Wales with an independent financial backer, sought a more hands-on role for clubs when it came to organising tournaments and they took out a High Court action against the WRU.

Cardiff were spiritual allies of the leading clubs in England and there were constant reports that they wanted to join the Allied Dunbar Premiership. They denied them, but their refusal to commit themselves to the WRU, unlike the other seven sides in the division, created a vacuum. No one knew what was going on and the newspapers were full of speculation, creating a drip-drip effect which undermined any feelings of goodwill towards the game amongst the Welsh public. The game was writing a long suicide note and nobody seemed able to do anything to prevent it.

We were due to play at the Arms Park on the first Saturday after Christmas. The WRU had negotiated a television contract with the Welsh language station that season which made provision for a live match every Saturday. The problem was that it kicked off at 6 p.m. – not a popular time for spectators – but the seven premier division clubs who had signed up with the Union had no option but to comply with the demands of S4C.

Cardiff, however, did not consider themselves to be bound by anything because they had not signed with the WRU and were not therefore receiving any of S4C's money. As a result, when they were asked to move the kick-off of our match back to 6 p.m., they refused and instead asked Pontypridd to turn up for a 2.30 p.m. start. Pontypridd had for years played Cardiff at the Arms Park on Boxing Day and it evolved to become one of the best-supported club matches in the Welsh calendar. The crowds at Pontypridd had held up despite the recession suffered by most of the other leading clubs in Wales and Cardiff would have enjoyed a healthy gate despite the evening kick-off, but they dragged Pontypridd into their dispute with the Union.

Pontypridd said they would turn up for the match when requested by the WRU, and we were told that it would start at 6 p.m. and that if we turned up in the afternoon there would be no referee or touch judges. This went on for days and days. Instead of looking forward to a match between two of the top clubs in Wales, all supporters had to read about was politicking.

It was only a few days before the match that Cardiff relented and agreed to play in the evening, but by then the damage had been done. Pontypridd followers I knew had arranged to do other things and the whole episode was depressing at a time when the Welsh game had so much to do to win the hearts and minds of young and old alike. We needed to attract new spectators and rekindle the interest of those who had stopped watching matches.

Ironically, the match was postponed because of torrential rain. Cardiff reckoned their pitch was playable, but the rebuilding work going on at the National Stadium had caused Cardiff's main stand to be flooded out – which meant, ironically, that the WRU had been the reason the game was called off. It turned out to be the turning point in our bid to become the first side to retain the Welsh championship. Cardiff were then going through a lean patch, but by the time the game was rearranged they had emerged as the main challengers to Swansea.

It was during this time that I first spoke to Bath. They had made it to the final of the Heineken Cup and they were a club with a significant Welsh connection. Ieuan Evans, Richard Webster and Nathan Thomas, all players I had played international rugby with, were in the Bath squad and they thrived on the competitive edge the Allied Dunbar Premiership had generated.

When I was growing up, there was nothing to compare with Welsh club rugby. It was hard and uncompromising and it had a wide foundation. Clubs like Pontypool, Maesteg, Aberavon and Newbridge were not places to visit on a wet Wednesday night, but ever since leagues were introduced in Wales in 1990 the effect has been to reduce the number of clubs at the top. We have a premier division of eight, but only four have a chance of winning the title at the start of the season.

English rugby has moved in the opposite direction and that appealed to me when I spoke to Bath. Cath and I were getting married that summer, and the added attraction of Bath, against a club like Saracens, was that we would not have had to move house. As a player, what concerns you more than anything else is the playing of the game. I was depressed with the state of rugby in Wales. It was crumbling into nothing, but those charged with running the game seemed to be unable to resolve personal differences in order to attempt to put things right.

All we had at Pontypridd was 14 league fixtures, a mixed bag called the Challenge Trophy, which involved teams from abroad –

many of them unheard of – taking part in a tournament they could not win, and the Swalec Cup. There was also Europe, the Heineken Cup and the European Conference, but the English clubs had threatened to boycott those tournaments because, they argued, they were run in favour of Wales, Scotland and Ireland when the two dominant forces were England and France. They wanted to take charge.

My heart told me to stay at Pontypridd, but my head said I would be a fool to turn Bath down. My contract with Pontypridd was due to end in the summer, although I had one with the WRU which ran until the end of the 1999 World Cup. The Union threatened to hold me to it and demand a transfer fee if I was intent on going to Bath, but that seemed to me to be a narrow-minded stance. I had won 57 caps for Wales and had given a lot for my country.

It was not as if I wanted to move for money, because I was not going to earn any more with Bath. WRU members are quick enough to criticise at dinners when they are emboldened by alcohol, saying that I should have done this or that, but my argument about the Bath offer was that I would clearly be playing at a higher level week in, week out. What was the Union going to guarantee as far as the club fixture list was concerned for the 1998–99 season? Were Cardiff going to be part of the set-up?

There were no answers, and Bath offered me a way out. There was no way my playing in England was going to make me a worse player for Wales, but as the weeks went on the WRU's position became more entrenched until Bath started being linked with other outside halves, in particular Thomas Castaignède of France who gave me the runaround at Wembley at the end of the 1998 Five Nations.

All I wanted to do was play club rugby to the highest possible standard. I had no argument with Pontypridd, a club to whom I owed so much, but I was being held hostage by the WRU, a union which had contributed so much to the decline of Welsh rugby in the previous ten years. You could understand Cardiff's frustration; it was shared by all the leading clubs, but only Cardiff had independent means of support.

I could not see how the WRU and the clubs were going to resolve their differences or sort out the huge problems which were besetting the game. English rugby appeared almost as divided, but at least the Allied Dunbar Premiership had a depth and a vibrancy which the Welsh league lacked. The English media had discovered rugby and the game was being hyped up.

It struck me that to become a part of it was almost like playing in Wales in the years gone by. The WRU wanted to keep its leading players in Wales, but all it could offer was money. When it came to rugby, it had less and less to offer as the months went by. Perhaps I should have joined Sheffield. All I wanted was to play rugby at the highest possible level, but a consequence of professionalism is that you are not master of your own destiny – until you are out of contract. Nothing would ever replace the days of working for my father, but as the 1997–98 season drew to a close, I was as concerned about my sense of disillusionment as I was about my form.

CHAPTER THIRTEEN

Bouncing Back

Kevin Bowring became Wales's sixth coach in seven years when he took over at the end of 1995, but he was the first to receive a salary. Various names had been aired by the media, including Ian McGeechan and Pierre Villepreux, but the WRU decided to keep the position Welsh. Kevin at least had a security denied to his predecessors, a contract, but there was no doubting the enormity of the task which lay ahead of him.

There were two essential aims: to improve our record against the emerging nations and ensure that recent defeats against countries like Canada and Western Samoa did not happen again, and to prevent the leading teams, which included England and France, from pulling further ahead of us. Kevin knew most of the players because of his involvement at the Under-21 and A levels and he deserved his chance.

He placed considerable emphasis on the individual in an era of conformity. His training sessions were varied and he stressed the importance of enjoyment through which, he believed, came fulfilment. His first international in charge saw Fiji visit the National Stadium but at that stage he was acting in a caretaker capacity after Alex Evans had declared his reign had come to an end. Kevin was, in effect, on trial, something the players were conscious of.

We started well, but they finished strongly and we had to hang on for a 19–15 victory. We had had more of the game and should have won by more, but it was the start of another era and we were under our third coach in eight months. There were understandable signs of uncertainty but we also showed what we were capable of and we moved the ball well despite the wet conditions.

We could look forward to the Five Nations with confidence, but fate intervened and I sat out the first three matches. I had been reasonably fortunate with injuries, but when Pontypridd went to Ebbw Vale at the end of 1995 I took a knock on my shoulder in the opening quarter. It became progressively sore, but I played on. I could hardly move it after the match and went to hospital for an X-ray.

No break was detected, which amazed me. Bruising was diagnosed and I carried on training, but every time I had a knock on it I was in agony. I played in our cup tie at Llanharan but wore a pad and tried to take contact on the other shoulder. The match was a romp – we won 102–5 – and I survived unscathed, but it was clear to me that something was seriously wrong. I went for another X-ray and this time a big crack was detected in the collar-bone.

I was angry that it had taken two weeks to find out what I already knew and it meant I had no chance of being fit for Wales's next international, against Italy the following month. I was also doubtful for the start of the championship. At least I could let my hair down at Christmas, for once, but it was little consolation. With a new coach at the helm you are anxious to make an instant impression, but I had to kick my heels while Arwel Thomas was given his first taste of international rugby.

Arwel had seemed destined to play for Wales ever since he had started playing for Neath, where he evoked memories of Barry John and Jonathan Davies. A slight figure, he had the touch of arrogance and devil which the Welsh look for in an outside half. He had moved from Neath to Bristol, starting a trend, although he was to join Swansea the following season. Arwel made his début against Italy in Cardiff and played his part in a victory which was more comfortable than the 31–26 scoreline suggested.

Arwel was one of five new caps in the side as Kevin showed his attacking intentions. Leigh Davies, the 19-year-old Neath centre in his first season of senior rugby, was a powerful threat in midfield, Arwel was a running outside half, Andrew Lewis was one of the most mobile props in Wales and Gwyn Jones was an open-side flanker in the mould of old: fast and fearless. Kevin wanted a game played at a sustained pace, based on width and support, and it went well for the first hour against Italy when we led 31–6.

I was not in the frame for the opening championship match against England at Twickenham, but Kevin showed his faith in me when I was chosen as a replacement. I do not like to think what would have happened had I had to go on after just a couple of minutes, but after that I recovered my match fitness with Pontypridd and remained on the bench against Scotland and Ireland. We were unfortunate to lose to the Scots. The team won plaudits for the manner of the performance, but there was only criticism after Dublin where we lost 30–17 to a team which two weeks before had been mauled by France.

It was a rare result in the recent history of fixtures between Wales and Ireland: a win for the home side. Any thoughts of revenge we had for our World Cup exit the previous year were banished in the opening quarter when the Irish started in their inimitable style, fire and fury, and we could not hold them. Arwel's honeymoon was over: he was shaken up after five minutes when he fielded a garryowen and took a knock on the head as an Irish horde enveloped him.

He became disorientated for a while and Kevin told me to warm up. Rugby union had yet to allow substitutes to be used and you were only allowed on to the field to replace an injured player, but coaches were able to inform someone they wanted to replace that they had just pulled a hamstring. Arwel battled on, but he was having one of those days when the more he tried to put things right, the more he made them worse. Kevin was torn between taking him off and letting Arwel battle back to form. I was up and down from my seat like a yo-yo.

'Warm up – you will be on soon,' Kevin would say. He would change his mind, then tell me to warm up again, and so it would go on. I stayed on the bench and Arwel was given a roasting by the media. I sat next to him on the coach as it left the ground to tell him what to expect. He was down, but his nature meant he would bounce back. Even though I would have been a substitute, I felt I should have gone on that day. An international against Ireland in Dublin is rarely an afternoon for the connoisseur; it is about pumping legs, rib-crunching tackles, bursting lungs and instant decision-making. To beat Ireland, you have to match their intensity in that opening period and not worry about living up to an ideal.

Arwel, the all-conquering hero two months before, was pilloried by the fickle Welsh public in an outburst of outrage only reserved for outside halves. We had one championship match in which to prevent our second consecutive whitewash. It would have been a poor return for the rugby we had played against England and Scotland, but this was the professional era. Excuses counted for nothing. Results were everything.

I was desperate to play and I had proved my form with Ponty-pridd. I knew I had a chance because of Arwel's misfortune but Kevin, like Alan Davies before him, set great store on loyalty. He was not going to make the mistake of the past by discarding someone after one below-par performance, but with me he had the fall-back that I would have been in the side but for injury. Now that I was fully fit, I was reclaiming what was mine.

Principles are all very well, but they are often sacrificed to expediency. Kevin needed a win even if his position was not in any danger. We needed to show that we had improved from 1995, and we were going to Australia in the summer. In his first couple of years Kevin was able to talk more about performances than results because of what he had inherited and because the next World Cup was in the distance, but given the tendency of the WRU to fire coaches in the build-up to a World Cup campaign he did not have as long as everyone supposed.

We had to beat France to ensure that we bottled the essence of what had been an enterprising campaign. After we had returned from Dublin, I came home one night to find a message on my answer-machine. It was from Kevin: would I give him a ring? I dallied before picking up the telephone. I was nervous, as if I was going to ask someone out on a date.

Kevin's first words were that he had picked the side to face France and I thought he was looking for a way to tell me bad news. He stuttered a bit before saying that he had decided to give me my chance. The rest of his words were lost to me: it was like winning my first cap again. I felt for Arwel because I knew what he was going through, but it had been a frustrating season for me and I wanted to finish it on a high.

The week before the international, I played for Pontypridd at Abertillery. We won easily, but I needed 12 stitches in a wound near my eye after a clash of heads. I must have looked like a French forward when the international match started, all battered and bruised, and only a few minutes had gone when Jean-Michel

Gonzalez decided to play doctor. It was typical France, looking to reopen old wounds – both literally and figuratively!

France needed to win to take the championship. Defeat would let in England, but that was the least of our concerns. We played with enterprise, as shown by Robert Howley's marvellous individual try when he sprinted 25 yards down the blind side, and a fierce determination, which allowed us to hold firm when France fought back at the end. We won 16–15 and I kicked the winning penalty after France had nosed their way in front with a typically slick try. The scenes were similar to those when we defeated England in 1993. There was a massive outpouring of relief, and a win was the least we deserved for a campaign which was a considerable improvement on 1995.

Australia beckoned, but at least we were not the rabble we had been five years previously. The management of Kevin and the WRU's rugby director Terry Cobner let the players know that we had to make up for 1991 in the way we conducted ourselves off the field. There was no way we could be any worse on it, and whereas the Wallabies had been at their peak during the earlier tour, they had failed to make the semi-finals of the 1995 World Cup.

We had another rude awakening. We started with a 62–20 victory over Western Australia in Perth, but three days later we faced ACT, a team which had changed considerably from the one we had defeated in 1991. The province was then a distant third in Australia behind Queensland and New South Wales, but it had been absorbed into the Super 12 series, which had taken over from the Super 10, and the Australian Rugby Union had ensured the side would thrive by giving it the means to import a number of established Wallabies.

We did reasonably well for an hour and were only 24–23 behind at the interval, but whereas they were able to play at a fast pace for 80 minutes, we blew up in the final quarter and ended up losing 69–30. It showed how rugby union had changed, embracing as it did elements of rugby league and American football. We were lacking not just in size but in fitness, conditioning and preparation. Our club scene in Wales was light years away from the Super 12, and we had to make too big a jump from club to international level.

We were heavily defeated in both Tests. We rallied in the first from 42–6 down to lose 56–25 and score three tries, but in the next international Kevin decided to employ a more limited game-plan. We hung on for 35 minutes before a moment of inspiration by Australia's full-back Matt Burke and we were hanging on after that. We lost 42–3 and at no stage looked to impose ourselves in attack.

I was surprised at the tactical change of emphasis, but it was Kevin's first real taste of international rugby outside Wales. I think he was surprised at what he found – just how far Wales had fallen behind – and it was at that point he probably appreciated the helplessness of his own position. What could the national coach of Wales do when a country like Australia, which boasted rugby union as only its nineteenth most popular sport, had moved so far ahead but was still lagging behind New Zealand and South Africa?

Kevin changed after Australia. When we went to Rome to play Italy that November we were encouraged to run only in certain areas of the field. Results had become important again, certainly when it came to matches you were expected to win, and the selection policy changed. Rugby league players returned, such as Scott Gibbs, Scott Quinnell, Allan Bateman and David Young to follow Jonathan Davies, but there was more of a reaction to defeats than there had been at the start of Kevin's reign, a trend that was to become increasingly apparent until his departure at the end of the 1998 championship season.

Before 1996 ended, I had been moved from outside half to full-back, a position where I had only played once. I had played the first three internationals of the new campaign – against the Barbarians, a festival match which did not merit the awarding of caps, and midweek friendlies against France and Italy – at outside half, but I was dropped from the side to face Australia that December.

I had come back from Australia knowing that I had to put more weight on. Australia, unlike Wales, is an outdoor nation, which helps when it comes to size. They had been too big and strong for us and I relished the chance to play against them in Cardiff. I was sacrificed, for reasons I still do not know, for Jonathan Davies, a decision which was popular at the box office but which made no sense to me.

Had I been replaced by Arwel, I would not have had a problem. He had made an impact with Swansea and he offered something different from me, but Jonathan had struggled to make the readjustment to rugby union since joining Cardiff. I will always rate Jonathan as one of the greatest players I ever had the privilege of watching, but his best days had gone, as he himself had admitted. To me, Kevin's selection of him sent out the wrong signals. Allan Lewis had stood down as the Wales backs coach. He never said anything publicly, but I know he was not happy with the decision to kick more than run in Rome and he had not played a central role tactically in Australia.

I felt I had got the back-line going well in recent matches and I had been playing well with Pontypridd. Age had caught up with Jonathan, and when Pontypridd played Cardiff at the National Stadium at the turn of the year I made sure that I made my point. We thrashed them in a match which convinced us that the first division title was ours if we kept our heads. My concern was that I had reached an age when I should either be at outside half on merit or not involved, but because of my goal-kicking I was always going to be a movable feast, and I found it frustrating.

As it was, I played most of the match against Australia because the full-back Wayne Proctor sustained an early injury and I replaced him. We only lost 28–19 but, looking back, it was probably the beginning of the end for Kevin. The confidence in his own beliefs and principles, which had fortified him at the start, was replaced by uncertainty. Consistency in selection became a thing of the past and we started to lose sight of what we were trying to achieve. Australia, despite the scoreline, were still a long way ahead of us.

It was difficult for Kevin because, like the many managers of Manchester City in recent years, he was judged not by what he had inherited but by the glory years of long before. The differences between the leading clubs in Wales and the WRU became more and more bitter, and although the Union created a national directorate based at Cardiff Institute where Kevin and Terry Cobner had their offices, players became caught in the tug-of-war between club and country. We trained with Wales four days a week in the 1996–97 while clubs got to grips with the implications of professionalism in terms of full-time players and preparation, but it meant having to train with our clubs in the evenings and the result was that we were tired mentally and physically long before the end of the season.

You needed to be injured to get a rest, which is what happened to me. Our championship campaign had started with a flourish in Edinburgh, where we defeated Scotland at Murrayfield for the first time in 12 years. I was still at full-back, having been chosen to play there against South Africa the previous December. Jonathan was originally chosen at outside half but withdrew with flu and was replaced by Arwel. The Springboks defeated us 37–20, but we played a more open game than we had in Italy and against Romania, and we took the initiative against Scotland.

With Gibbs, Bateman, Young and Quinnell back in the side, we were too strong for Scotland. I scored 19 points, including a try, to pass 500 points in international rugby and we won by an impressive 34–19, thanks to a purple period in the second half. The victory set us up for Ireland in Cardiff: surely another jinx would be broken?

We started with a try in the first minute and we expected to go on from there, but we allowed them back in and they scored a try after a garryowen by Eric Elwood had me in difficulties on my own line. It was a swirling kick, and as I moved to get under it I ended up dabbing the ball against the goalpost and it squirted over the line for Jonathan Bell to touch it down and claim a try. I thought the post was one of my players but I did not think it was a fair try, a belief which television replays confirmed. Bell had been offside.

Ireland pulled further ahead, and although we rallied in the second half we lost by a point, as we had in the 1995 World Cup. They had been typically Irish, swarming around Scott Gibbs in the midfield and preventing us from getting the ball wide. We had not been aware enough tactically and we had missed the injured Allan Bateman in the centre. We should have been lining up a Triple Crown showdown with England but instead had to mount a salvage operation against France in Paris.

It was our last match at the Parc des Princes – not that we would mourn its passing as an international rugby ground – just as the international against England was to be the last played at the National Stadium before it was rebuilt for the 1999 World Cup. We should have beaten France: we took the game to them, but again the match turned on a kick I had to field.

The replacement outside half David Aucagne tried a drop goal which went horribly wide. As I ran to catch it, I was aware that I was not going to get there in time and I let it bounce. The ground was hard and it soared over my head and into the arms of Christophe Lamaison, who sent his wing Laurent Leflamand away. I was criticised afterwards for not catching the ball, but it was out of my reach, and all credit to Lamaison for chasing what had seemed a lost cause. We lost 27–22, but we had recaptured our attacking verve. It was not to last, however, and that warm, springlike day in Paris marked the high point of the Bowring era. For me, though, the biggest peak of all still had to be scaled.

CHAPTER FOURTEEN

This Mortal Coil

By the time we played England, speculation about the 35-strong squad which would tour South Africa with the Lions in the summer had reached fever pitch. I had been included in the preliminary squad of 62, and although I was not happy about playing at full-back for Wales, I knew it would do my prospects of being chosen by the Lions no harm. Having also played at centre in international rugby, I offered a versatility touring sides invariably look for.

Rugby union may now be a professional sport with players bound to the club which holds their contracts, but being selected for the Lions is still the ultimate honour for any British or Irish player. Money has not sullied the importance of the Lions but has enhanced it, as the South Africans, counting their rands, were only too happy to acknowledge. One of the reasons I had turned down approaches from rugby league clubs was that I wanted to go on a Lions tour, but I did not hold out much hope at the start of the 1996–97 season.

When I was dropped for the international against Australia I despaired, but the Lions coach Ian McGeechan had said how important goal-kicking would be in South Africa. Pontypridd were flying high and I felt I deserved a run in the Wales side. Moving to full-back might have been my salvation as far as making it to South Africa was concerned, but it was difficult adjusting to the position. At outside half, you are involved in the game all the time. Full-back is a more lonely position. I was fortunate to have the experienced Ieuan Evans on one of my wings with Wales. He nursed me through matches, especially when it came to positioning in defence. I was never going to explode into the line in the manner of Matt Burke or Christian Cullen, and I was never really sure why I had been chosen there, my goal-kicking apart. Ever since Mike Rayer had lost his place through injury, the position had been a problem one for Wales. My predecessor, Wayne Proctor, was a wing, while Tony Clement was injured. Some observers found it hard to square Wales's stated preference for a running game with my presence at full-back.

After we had pushed France close in Paris, Fran Cotton, the Lions manager, came into our dressing-room to congratulate us on our performance. I had played that day with a gumshield, the first time I had ever worn one, having broken a bone in my mouth at Caerphilly the previous week. I would have pulled out, but I knew the Lions selectors were now looking at players in earnest. I could not afford to be on the sidelines.

As fortune would have it, the first player to head my way was the giant second row Olivier Merle, a 20-stone bruiser who was not blessed with a sidestep. I knew he was going to look to run straight through me, and he shoved his elbow straight into my face on his way to the line. The gumshield did its job, but I wish the French would lose their obsession with reconstructing my face.

Injury is an occupational hazard. It does not discriminate: you can be David Campese or Jonah Lomu, or Dai Jones playing for your local village third team – fit one minute, out of action the next. Injury is a reminder of your mortality and a reason why you should savour the good times. Our final championship match of the 1997 campaign should have been a moment of personal triumph for me: it was my 50th cap for Wales and I had become the youngest player in the history of the international game to achieve the feat, beating Philippe Sella's record by nine months. Ten minutes after the start, however, I was on my way to hospital. Phil de Glanville made a break and I tackled him. He offloaded the ball but it went loose and I dived on it with my arm stretched out. England's flanker Richard Hill came in and caught my arm accidentally with his boot. I felt a sharp pain and my elbow went dead.

Mark Davies, the Wales physiotherapist who was going to South Africa with the Lions, came on and made a quick inspection. 'Carcass', as Mark is known, normally tells an injured player that there is nothing seriously wrong and to get on with it, but he poured cold water on my arm and said I should give it a couple of minutes. I knew then I had a problem. I jogged back to my position and could feel something squelching around in my arm. I prayed that England did not hoist a garryowen, because I would have had to catch it with one hand. We were awarded a penalty and Jonathan Humphreys called me up to kick at goal. I told him I had broken my arm and he looked at me in bemusement.

It was to be Humph's last match as Wales skipper after a two-year stint. He had taken considerable public criticism, but he never let it get to him. He gave his all for his country and for his club, Cardiff. Some of the comments about him were personal and deeply insulting, and I could not understand them. He never claimed to be the best player in the world, but he had a huge heart and I had a lot of time for him. I also knew what he was going through.

The sand arrived for me to take the kick but I could not mould it with both hands and had to use my right. I could not put any power into the kick either, and it dropped well short. I signalled to the bench that I had to come off. A doctor examined my arm and pronounced it broken. It was off to Cardiff Royal Infirmary for an X-ray with the threat, much to my dread, of an operation. It was going to be a day to remember for all the wrong reasons.

As it turned out, fate worked in my favour. England turned us over and took advantage of the fact that we had been ravaged by injury. Had I remained on the field I would have been overworked in defence, and bearing in mind what was to happen at Twicken-ham the following year it was probably no bad thing that I was absent.

Not that I thought so at the time. I was proving a less than model patient at the hospital. The nurses wanted to cut off my jersey but I said no way, it was my 50th and it was staying in one piece. Have it your way, they said, but do not complain about the pain. I screamed out in agony as the jersey was manoeuvred off me and underneath was my lucky T-shirt which I also wanted to keep. Cath took one look at it and declared that it was lucky no more. It was ripped off me and thrown in the bin.

The X-ray showed that I had broken my arm. The break was a clear one and there was a large gap which had to be pinned. I was also told I would have to have another X-ray to see if I had broken my elbow. My patience had gone by now and I told the nurses there was nothing wrong with it. As far as I was concerned, any hope I had of going to South Africa had vanished and I just wanted to be left alone. I was due to be flying out with Wales to the Hong Kong Sevens the following day, but instead I was going to go under the knife in a Swansea hospital.

I went back to the team hotel later that night, and the WRU weren't exactly sympathetic. They wanted my Hong Kong kit back: three T-shirts, a tracksuit and a pair of shorts. I said I had left it at home and they could not have it back. I had missed the presentation of my 50th cap at the dinner, my Lions hopes had nose-dived, I was not going to be able to lift the championship trophy aloft for Pontypridd and all the WRU were concerned about was a few items of kit. No chance.

I tried to talk my way out of having the operation, but I was wasting my time. The doctor did not mince his words: he told me that I would be out of action for a long time and that I would probably not make South Africa. The last thing I remember before the injection took effect is looking out at the hospital field and saying that I remembered playing on it. The next thing I knew, I was being slapped awake with the highlights of the England match being shown on the television.

Malcolm Downes, a surgeon who had worked with the Wales team and who was based at the hospital, came to see me, and he confirmed the original diagnosis: that I would be fortunate to be playing within four months. I had less than eight weeks to prove my fitness for South Africa – assuming I was selected. I saw the surgeon who operated on me, Bob Leyshon, and he also said that time was against me. I asked him, if I had the slightest chance of making it, to say that to the Lions selectors.

Derek Quinnell was the Lions' adviser based in Wales and he would telephone occasionally to see how I was. I had the plaster removed after ten days and the stitches shortly afterwards, which allowed me to resume full fitness work. I knew my chances of making it were slim, but Pontypridd were contacted by a woman called Nicki Bateman who lived in Wimbledon. She had read about my plight and asked whether the club was interested in her treatment, which involved sticking my hand in a magnetic coil three times a day. Nicki reckoned it would increase my recovery time by at least three weeks, and I was only too happy to give it a go. Nicki spent six weeks in South Wales, with Pontypridd picking up the bill. It was typical of the club: there was no chance that I would be helping in the quest for our first league title, but they were prepared to help me in any way they could. I used to spend three hours a day with my arm in the magnetic coil and Pontypridd did not want anything to be said in public about the treatment, not even when the coil was taken with me to Llanelli for a crucial league game.

On the day the Lions squad was announced, Cath and I were going to the Ideal Homes Exhibition in London. The players who were going to South Africa were to be informed by letter, so I hoped the mail would come before we left for the train. It did and Cath picked it up. She said there was nothing from the Lions, just a letter from a firm of solicitors. I took that to be about an impending court case I was involved in following an incident in a Swansea nightclub earlier in the year. She opened the letter and I asked, fairly forlornly, what it was about. She put on a face and then burst out laughing: 'Only that you are to spend two months in South Africa.'

It took some moments to sink in, not just because of my injury but because this was the pinnacle of my ambition, what I had worked so hard for. I called my parents because I had promised them that if I made the squad I would pay for them to watch the Test series. All I had to prove was that I was fit to travel, and the Lions organised a week's training in Weybridge shortly before leaving for South Africa.

I worked hard at Pontypridd, but shortly before leaving for Weybridge I damaged my calf during a sprints routine. It meant that it was not until the third day of the Lions' training camp that I had to do any contact work. By then my arm was ready to take it, and after I had come through a physical 40 minutes I bore a smile a mile wide. I do not know if Nicki Bateman's coil made the difference, but it certainly did me no harm. I had defied medical opinion and I will always be grateful to her.

Not everyone survived the week. The Irish prop Peter Clohessy had a bad back and everyone felt his distress when he realised he was not going to make it. Paul Wallace replaced him and went on to have an outstanding tour. One man's misfortune is another man's opportunity.

The management was concerned as much with squad bonding

as with training during the week at Weybridge. The concept of the Lions is unique, players from four different rugby-playing nations coming together for a tour abroad. We were encouraged immediately not to think of ourselves as Welsh, Scottish, Irish or English: we were Lions, and the rooms were organised so that everyone shared with someone of a different nationality – which for the Celts invariably meant an Englishman.

My first room-mate was Northampton's Nick Beal. I had last come across him during an Under-11 match between East Wales and West Wales at the National Stadium. I remembered him well: he had been the West's best player, a big, powerful wing who had given us the runaround. National barriers were trampled down immediately and friendships were formed for life with players you had only been on nodding terms with before. I am in regular contact now with England's Matt Dawson, Scotland's Gregor Townsend and Ireland's Keith Wood.

At the end of the Weybridge week we went into the town for a few beers. I have always believed in training and playing hard and then relaxing one night a week. It is how we forged such a close spirit at Pontypridd, although in the early years the nights out amounted to a few more than one a week. You are more than team-mates: you are friends, close friends, and you would do anything for each other. As the French clubs were to find out in the Heineken Cup, hit one Pontypridd player and you hit us all. I think a few of the Lions were a little surprised at the enthusiasm I showed for liquid refreshment after matches, but rugby union has always been about more than just the 80 minutes – and long may that continue.

I suppose I am a bit of a dietician's nightmare. I am addicted to chocolate and the Lions' fitness adviser Dave McLean would go mad with me. I enjoyed it when we were staying in Cape Town: the hotel was close to the ground and was just a few yards away from a shopping centre which included a magnificent sweet shop. I had to watch out for Dave before sneaking in there. Not drinking alcohol in the week before a game is no problem, but I cannot do without my chocolate.

Ian McGeechan addressed us at the end of the Weybridge week. He wanted nothing but total effort and he warned us that we would be followed by the largest media circus we would ever see. We would need to watch what we did and what we said. Players were invited to react to certain questions. Doddie Weir, the big Scotland second row, was told: 'You were seen coming out of a nightclub at 4 a.m., just hours before a big match. What do you have to say for yourself?' Quick as a flash, Doddie had an answer: 'Mistaken identity. It must have been my father.'

An attentive media was nothing new to me. Wales is like a small village where there are no secrets, but what was different was the expectancy we travelled with. Wales touring New Zealand, Australia or South Africa has little significance in world terms – brave words, foregone conclusions – but the Lions were different. For the first time in my career, I could compete with one of rugby's leading nations on an equal basis.

I had looked a sight with my arm stuck in Nicki Bateman's magnetic coil, but I have never cared about appearances. The two-month rest had left me fresh for what I knew were going to be the two most demanding months of my career. If making the squad had been hard enough, getting into the Test team was going to require even more application. This was the ultimate honour – and we were being paid. I would happily have paid my own way.

CHAPTER FIFTEEN

Wounded Knee

South Africa was like Wales in the 1970s. Success had bred arrogance, and we had no sooner arrived at our first hotel outside Durban than we were reading that the series was a formality. South Africa were going to win all three internationals; the Lions were nothing more than England with a pinch of Celtic seasoning. The Springboks had only once lost a series to the Lions, way back in 1974.

Ian McGeechan and Fran Cotton had played in all four Tests that year, while Jim Telfer, the assistant coach who had responsibility for the forwards, was on the 1968 tour of South Africa. We had a management which knew what it took to beat the Springboks and what struck me immediately, as a player who was used to being on the wrong end of several hidings with Wales, was how focused the three were. They were blessed with a cool but steely determination and they were a perfect blend.

Geech was a supreme tactician who had worked everything out in advance. He knew we were never going to match South Africa for size and everything in training was geared to moving their players around, popping the ball at the point of contact and supporting. It demanded supreme fitness and concentration and Geech was not one to holler and remonstrate. He was like a chess Grand Master, calculating every move, and he knew he had the pieces to win.

Jim was far more of an extrovert. His job was to stoke up the forwards, and he did not need any prompting. He never let them ease up and I felt the sharp end of his tongue when it came to practising restarts. It did not matter if the wind was howling or it was pelting down with rain: the ball had to land exactly where he wanted. 'For ***** sake, Neil, put it on the button, where I say.' If I heard that once, I heard his craggy Scottish voice say it a thousand times. He had a profound influence on our success. He did not so much play the bad cop to Geech's good cop, but you knew as a player that if you messed up Jim would be on your case, and you need that.

You knew what the tour meant to them both. Jim had been the coach of the Lions in 1983 when they were whitewashed in New Zealand and the pain of that failure had not eased. This was his chance of putting that behind him, and whereas the 1983 squad had not been totally united, in 1997 every player put the needs of the team before his own aspirations.

Fran Cotton, the manager, made sure of that. Fran did not have a coaching role, nor did he ever attempt to interfere on the field. The players were treated like adults and we made sure we were not distracted by having to go here, there and everywhere in our spare time. The Wales tours I had been on had been marred by a welter of minutiae: wear this in the morning, that in the afternoon, go here in the evening, don't do this, don't do that. It was like being on a school trip. In South Africa, however, the players were not saddled with a list of dos and don'ts. There was not even an alcohol ban before matches: if you wanted a pint the night before a match, there was nothing stopping you – except your sense of responsibility to yourself and to the squad, which the management fostered by the mature way they handled the players. They trusted us. Fran was a big man in every sense of the word and his part in our success was significant.

Geech wasted no time after we had checked into our first hotel in putting us through our paces. Training was hard and intense. He told us the provincial matches were warm-ups to the main event: the Test series. They offered the coaches the chance to try out combinations, and there was not a player on the trip who was not in contention for a Test place. Our first match was Eastern Province and I desperately wanted to play because it was 11 weeks since I had completed a game.

I was given my chance, but my rustiness was only too evident in the opening minutes. I sliced my first three attempted kicks to touch, even though the conditions were glorious. Most of the players were making their first appearances in a Lions jersey and there were a few nerves. We took time to settle, understandably, but when we found our rhythm we put together some exciting passages of play and ran out 39–11 winners. I only missed one kick at goal and we enjoyed a good night out afterwards. We had arrived. We were Lions.

I was on the bench for the second match against Border. The conditions were more like a wet Wednesday night in Pontypridd than the hard-baked grounds you associate with South Africa, but the players chiselled out a hard 18–14 victory. It was the first and last match for the England outside half Paul Grayson, who aggravated a leg injury and became the second casualty of the tour after Peter Clohessy. We all felt the pain of his disappointment.

His absence gave me the chance to play at outside half the following week, although I was aware that that was not going to be the position where I was going to be challenging for a Test place, because Paul's replacement was Mike Catt, his rival for the England outside-half jersey. We played Western Province after Border at Newlands, the venue for the first Test. I was again on the bench, much to my disappointment, and Tim Stimpson continued at full-back. He had worked hard on his goal-kicking and it showed, as he kicked 18 points in an impressive 38–21 victory.

The South African media had been quiet after our first two matches, but they seized on an incident during the game between the two wings, South Africa's James Small and our John Bentley. They had had a few words after Small objected to being tackled by Bentos, and Small refused to shake hands afterwards. What hurt him most was that Bentos had scored two of our four tries and he squealed to journalists, claiming that he had been gouged. Fran whirred into action and swatted Small away. 'We are not here to massage James Small's ego,' was his response to demands for an inquiry. One-up to Bentos and the Lions.

Bentos emerged as one of the characters of the tour. He went everywhere armed with a camcorder, no doubt looking for the chance to earn £250 on *You've Been Framed*. He was an extrovert, a voluble northerner who had resurrected his Test career after returning from rugby league. He attracted more column inches in the South African press than virtually all the other players put together and was without doubt one of the stars of the tour. He once made the mistake of leaving his hotel bedroom door open.

Austin Healey was passing and heard Bentos on the telephone to his wife. 'You won't believe it, love,' he gushed. 'I am more famous here than I am at home.' Austin made sure all the squad knew about this within minutes. Bentos was the big wind-up merchant of the squad, but he learned to close his door when making telephone calls.

Three matches into the tour and we had a 100 per cent record. The next stop was a place I knew well: Witbank, scene of a Welsh humiliation less than two years earlier. South Eastern Transvaal had metamorphosed into Mpumalanga but most of the players were the same. This was a game I desperately wanted to play in and I had the added bonus of being given the outside-half jersey because of Paul's injury.

We slaughtered them. I scored one of our ten tries and it was a pleasure to be part of such a strong team. They had ridden roughshod over Wales in 1995, but they had no answer to the strength of the Lions' forwards or our pace behind. Our 64–14 victory made South Africa sit up: these were no toothless Lions.

The performance was marred by a sickening injury suffered by Doddie Weir, who was the victim of one of the most blatant acts of foul play I have ever seen on a rugby field. Mpumalanga's second row Marius Bosman, who had already taken exception to the try-scoring prowess of our flanker Rob Wainwright, launched a karate-style kick at Doddie's standing leg as he bent into a maul. Doddie collapsed in pain and had to be helped from the field. Not only was his tour over but his career was also threatened. Amazingly, Bosman remained on the field. He had been cleaned out by Doddie at the line-out and decided to exact retribution. It was a disgraceful act which should have been met by a lengthy suspension. There is no place in the game for a thug like that, but the South Africans were obviously grateful that Bosman had ended the tour of a player who was pushing hard for a Test place because he was only handed a fine and was allowed to carry on playing.

Contrast that with a few months later when, after being sent off playing for Pontypridd at Brive, the Wales number eight Dale McIntosh was hauled up before European Rugby Cup Ltd for putting his thumbs up to a jeering crowd as he left the field. Dale had already been banned for 30 days for his dismissal, which came after he had been set upon by four Frenchmen, and he faced the suspension being doubled.

It showed the absurdity that is modern rugby union in matters of discipline. The decision on Bosman should not have been left to the South African Union. The game has to shake off its amateur heritage and ensure that there are uniform punishments for all players who have committed acts of foul play. The inconsistencies are appallingly rife. What Bosman did with his reckless and wanton act was every bit as bad as the action of a biter. Doddie is fortunate to be able to walk, let alone play, again. Rugby is now a living for players at the top and the authorities have to ensure that the likes of Bosman are not given *carte blanche* to roam fields and end careers.

Fran went into overdrive but the South Africans hid behind a rule which said that, as the referee had seen the incident and taken action by awarding a penalty, their hands were tied. Bosman ended up being fined by the Mpumalanga union which should have thrown the book at him. The incident, and its aftermath, hardened our resolve. It was going to take more than an idiot to stop us.

The South Africans had their revenge the following game. We faced Northern Transvaal at Loftus Versfeld and it was our only provincial defeat of the tour. As the first Test loomed closer, there was a discernible tightening-up at forward. Jim was getting the pack to drive more and more and some of the backs, Jerry Guscott in particular, felt that we were having to move slow ball behind. We certainly started slowly against the Blue Bulls and at one stage we were 25–7 down.

It was the only day of the tour when I was not playing or on the bench. Tim Stimpson was at full-back and once again he kicked well. My prospects of making the Test team were starting to dim. I had not played against any of the leading provinces and there was only one more Saturday before the opening Test. Time was running out.

We fought back well against the Blue Bulls before losing 35–30. Scott Gibbs came on as a replacement, his first outing since injuring his ankle against Border. Scott was anxious to make up for lost time and he had only been on the field a few seconds when he crunched into their wing Grant Esterhuizen. He was cited for delivering an imagined forearm smash, a trifling incident compared to Bosman's kick.

Scott was summoned the following day to a citation hearing which was presided over by a High Court judge. The South

African judiciary is not noted for its ability to get things right and Scott, or Mr Gibbs, as he was addressed at the hearing, was suspended for one match. It was a kind of revenge for the Bosman outcry, but the judge got it wrong. He should have suspended Scott for the rest of the tour because Mr Gibbs was pumping himself up to become the man of the Test series. Judge Daniels ensured that motivation was not a problem.

The defeat meant that we had to get it right in the next two matches, against Gauteng Lions and Natal, which were potentially the toughest of the tour outside the internationals, although the provinces were not allowed to choose their current members of the South African squad. Gauteng Lions were the former Transvaal and it meant a return to Ellis Park, the ground where Wales's 1995 World Cup dream had died.

I was on the bench. Nick Beal was at full-back while Mike Catt had his first match of the tour, having arrived from England's tour of Argentina. The Gauteng players were up for it, not least two members of the South Africa World Cup-winning side who had since fallen out of favour: Hennie le Roux and Kobus Wiese. The Lions were a typically South African side, obsessed with establishing a physical supremacy at forward, but they were unable to match our fitness.

I replaced Tony Underwood with 23 minutes to go. We were trailing and Mike was struggling to find his kicking touch at altitude. I had not been on long when Austin Healey finished off a flowing move and I landed the conversion from the touchline to put us 10–9 ahead. It was my most important kick of the tour outside the Tests and Bentos then scored probably the best individual try of the tour, weaving in and out of tackles on a run in which he virtually doubled back on himself. He confused his support players as well as the defence and the only thing for him was to score, which he did. The Lions had tamed the Lions.

It was a seminal moment of the tour. The South African media had expected Gauteng to maul us, but we had matched them at forward and been far too strong for them in the final quarter. That was a feature of the tour, as we were to prove in the Tests. For all the hype about how quick the Super 12 series was and how there was nothing in British or Irish rugby to match it, we were far fitter than the South Africans. After Gauteng, we knew that we had the means to win the Test series.

Geech gave me my chance against Natal. It was a week before the first international but nothing was being read into the selection of the side. The back division was an all-Celtic affair with the Welsh quintet of me, Ieuan Evans, Allan Bateman, Scott Gibbs and Robert Howley supplemented by two Scots, Gregor Townsend and Alan Tait. South Africa had warmed up for the opening international by thrashing Tonga in the week, but little could be read into that game, which was their first under their new coach, Carel du Plessis.

I was up for Natal. They were led out by John Allan, the former Scotland and South Africa hooker, who was playing his last match for the Sharks before taking up a coaching job with London Scottish. He emerged from the tunnel alone and ran on to the field so quickly that he ended up on the opposite touchline before he knew it. He was pumped up to the eyeballs, but we were focused.

We took them apart in our most impressive display of the tour to date. We dominated the game and played some fluent rugby. What pleased me more than the nine kicks I landed in a match haul of 24 points was our play at restarts, a feature of the game which is lamentable in Wales. We took virtually every one, the hard work I had put in with kicking coach Dave Alred paying off. Jim's friendly words of advice also came to mind: 'On the button, Neil, on the button.'

The one deflating moment was the shoulder injury suffered by my Wales half-back partner Rob Howley, who followed Paul Grayson and Scott Quinnell home. Unlike the other two, Rob had been certain of a Test place and the pain in his eyes at the end of the match was piercing. Being chosen for a Lions tour is like being selected for the Olympics: it is something which only comes around every four years, and to be denied by injury is a cruel fate.

There was not much I could say to him. His family were preparing to fly out to South Africa when his shoulder went and Rob's injury was another reminder of how injuries are not discriminating. His only consolation was that he was young enough and good enough to make the 2001 Lions tour of New Zealand and South Africa, but he had been denied the chance of taking on South Africa scrum half Joost van der Westhuizen on equal terms to decide who was the leading scrum half in the world. Van der Westhuizen had scored three tries against Wales the previous December, but he had enjoyed a luxury ride courtesy of his forwards.

The squad embraced each other after the final whistle because we had not only vaulted an important hurdle but we had done so with a considerable amount to spare. The cocksure attitude of the South Africans which had greeted us on our arrival had given way to something approaching uncertainty. Suddenly the Test series was not the foregone conclusion it had once appeared. The hotel chain which put us up for the whole tour had an in-house magazine which contained an article predicting a whitewash for us. In South Africa, you are never denied the means for self-motivation.

CHAPTER SIXTEEN

Heaven's Gate

As the first Test loomed, so the nerves started building up. The first cause for anxiety was the announcement of the side, and the management decided to post a letter under the door of each player in the early hours of the Wednesday morning so that everyone would have a few moments to come to terms with whether he was in or out.

The alternative was to adopt the normal tour procedure and read out the side at a squad meeting. That can be a brutal experience for someone with high hopes of being selected who finds himself left out. There is no one you want to speak to until you have collected your thoughts and come to terms with your omission. At the same time as you are trying to pick up the pieces, others are beaming with delight. The decision to inform everyone by letter was a typically thoughtful move by the management. It was how we had learned of our original selections, and they wanted those who were omitted to congratulate the players who had been chosen ahead of them. It was easier to do that after a period of reflection.

I had no idea whether I would be chosen. The day before the letters were slipped under the players' doors we had soundly beaten the Emerging Springboks 51–22 in Wellington. Tim appeared at full-back and scored 26 points. He had progressed well on the tour and I felt there was little to choose between us. The fact that I had been rested in the match before the Test, or at least given a seat on the bench, was a good omen, but Tim took the opportunity to stake his claim. The management had not divided the squad into Saturday and midweek teams, partly to maintain unity but also because there was intense competition for places in most positions. In the end, there was no point in worrying, and I had a good night's sleep.

I was sharing a room with Tony Underwood, the Newcastle wing who had gone on the 1993 Lions tour to New Zealand. He had not played in any of the Tests, and he was up early in the morning to open his letter. He gave me the thumbs down and his hurt was obvious. I was delighted when he was chosen to play in the final Test because he proved on the tour that he was a player of the highest quality. Tony spent most of that day on his own. Alan Tait, the Scottish utility back, had been given the left-wing berth even though he had come on the tour primarily as a centre.

Tony asked me if I wanted to open my envelope but I preferred to lie in bed. I had reasoned that if Tony had been left out I had probably suffered the same fate, because on Wales tours Test players share rooms before an international. Tony slipped out of the room and I eventually plucked up the courage to find out whether it was time to smile or grimace. The message was simple and is as clear to me now as it was then: 'You have been chosen to play in the first Test against South Africa. Good luck.'

I was glad Tony had left the room because my delight would not have mixed well with his disappointment. I rang home. My mother wept with joy while my father, as dispassionate as ever, told me to make sure I set a new points-scoring record. They were flying out to South Africa the following day with Cath and her family but they were already flying high.

Tim Stimpson congratulated me in the breakfast room and he meant it. I would have had no arguments if he had been chosen ahead of me. He had had an excellent tour, and if at the start of it his natural talent as a full-back had been balanced by my ability to harvest points, his kicking had improved so significantly that there could not have been much between us at the moment of reckoning. Perhaps the fact that I had kicked goals in the heat of international competition tilted it my way, but Tim was to finish the tour as the highest scorer and he made the Test field when he came on as a replacement in the final international.

The three days before the Newlands Test passed quickly. I saw my parents the day before and my mother remarked on how ill I looked. I have always had a white complexion, but I was so nervous that I made an albino look ruddy. Thousands of British and Irish supporters had descended on Cape Town and I knew from my calls home just how much interest the Lions were generating in Wales.

Despite the relative failure of the Wales team since 1979, rugby remains the national sport of Wales. The public have been largely starved of success but, as they showed when filling Wembley three times in the 1997–98 season, their appetite for the game remains hearty. They took to the Lions, not least because there were a number of Welshmen in the squad, and pubs and clubs were packed on match days.

The night before the match, I went out to an Italian restaurant down the road from our hotel with Ieuan and Tom Smith, the Scotland prop. Tom was the quietest player in the squad, with very little to say for himself. We walked the few hundred yards in our tracksuits with passers-by wishing us well and passed a peaceful couple of hours. Tom and I were playing in our first Test for the Lions, but Ieuan was an old hand having been on the 1989 and 1993 tours and he was able to divert our minds away from rugby. Although it was to be Ieuan's last match because he picked up a groin injury the following day, Tom and I kept up the routine before the following two Tests.

Tom arrived in South Africa virtually unannounced and the Springboks could not quite believe it when he and Paul Wallace were chosen as the two props in the internationals. Ian McGeechan and Jim Telfer knew what they were doing, though. South Africa had two tall props, Os du Randt and Adrian Garvey, who would look to drive through their opponents. Tom and Paul burrowed underneath them and nullified the greater size and weight of their opponents. The scrummage, the virility symbol of South African rugby, was fused by a doughty Scotsman and a durable Irishman. God bless 'em.

I snatched only a few hours' sleep the night before the Test. It was going to be the biggest day of my life. Playing for Wales had always meant everything to me, but this was something else again. What made it even more special was that I was not going to go into a match against a powerful team like South Africa hoping that we could keep the score down. We were thinking about nothing but victory.

We had the advantage of being a settled touring side while South Africa, under new management, had only played one international. They were also expected to win, all the more so because the English beef which had been expected to underpin the side had been rejected, a sort of steak ta-ta. Only one Englishman was in the front five, the captain Martin Johnson, although the back row was all English after Tim Rodber came in to replace flu victim Eric Miller. Eric's joy at receiving a good-luck letter had been dashed when he succumbed to a virus. Tim grabbed his opportunity with both hands, but there had been no sense of superiority among the English players, even though they had long had the upper hand over the Celtic countries in the Five Nations. They took the decision not to meet fire with fire in the tight five but to seek to undermine the Springboks with stealth like men, and their commitment to the success of the tour never wavered, despite their personal disappointments.

I got up late on the day of the game to give my legs a rest. They felt like jelly anyway. I made sure Dave McLean was not around and tucked into beans and chips. I have never been able to get my head around dietary advice: I am not into greens and pasta. I wanted to stick to my normal routine to help keep the nerves at bay, but as the minutes ticked away the tension grew. Our hotel was only a short walk from the ground but we travelled by coach. As we got out to get our kit, we were surrounded by thousands of supporters. I looked for a familiar face but did not see one, but then I heard a familiar voice, shouting Pontypridd chants. It was Cath's father and it gave me a lift.

I was terrible in the dressing-room, literally sick with nerves. I was even whiter than the day before and at such moments you wonder why you put yourself through such an ordeal. I thought enviously of my friends sitting down to watch the match on television, their hands clasped around a pint glass with nothing to worry about except whether they had a good view. The changing-room was a cacophony of noise. Different players have different ways of winding themselves up. The likes of Ieuan and Jerry have a detached calm, but Jim was stoking up the forwards.

Lawrence Dallaglio strode around and reminded everyone what we were there for. Martin Johnson was a quiet captain, but when he spoke you listened. Keith Wood also had a lot to say, but for the most part the words were a way of releasing tension and helping the time pass. Our preparations were complete. We just wanted to get out there.

My first task was to kick off and I put the ball out of play on the full. I looked up to the skies and pleaded, 'Not today, of all days.' South Africa took the lead with an early penalty but I had the chance to equalise a few minutes later. As fate would have it, the kick was from virtually the same spot where I had practised the previous Thursday. I had missed every one because my left foot had slipped on the soft ground as I was about to kick. I took a number of deep breaths and resolved to ram my left foot down hard. I had never been so relieved to see a kick go over. The pressure was lifted, the nerves were gone. I started to revel in the moment.

The match went as we expected it to. The Springboks looked to ram home their perceived physical superiority, but the more they failed, the more they tried. They did not play with much intelligence and threw away a winning position. We led 9–8 at half-time and went 12–8 ahead shortly after the interval when I kicked my fourth penalty. The South Africans then scored a try after Scott Gibbs, of all players, had missed a tackle. That incident apart, he had a massive match, dumping a number of Springboks on their backsides, shattering the myth of their physical invincibility.

At 16–12 down with 20 minutes to go, we were still confident of winning. I kicked another penalty and they had a try disallowed for a forward pass. As in the provincial matches, we were finishing the stronger, and with ten minutes to go Matt Dawson, playing instead of Rob Howley, scored the try of his life, one of which Rob would have been proud. He sold two outrageous dummies as he broke from a scrum and four tacklers stopped as Matt streaked 25 yards to the line. South Africa's preparations had been based on dealing with Rob and Matt was something of an unknown character. His try was the old schoolboy dummy which had 'see you' written all over it, but he had twice before exposed Ruben Kruger on South Africa's open side. It was a try worthy of winning the game, but there was more to come.

The Springboks were shaken but they had little more to give. My conversion had hit the post, but we were soon back on the attack. Scott took the ball up and ran over a couple of defenders. Tim Rodber took the ball on and passed it to me. I could see the line and started celebrating the try, but I saw Henry Honiball streaking across and quickly passed to Alan Tait, who claimed the five points. We had done it.

The joy was unconfined. Those who were not playing jumped off the bench and everyone celebrated. It was a special moment for the whole squad. Martin Johnson made sure no one got carried away by saying we had won only a battle, not the war, but we had shown the South Africans we were not the whipping boys we had been billed as. One newspaper billboard outside the ground read 'Lions in town: the Pansies have arrived'. Flower power had held sway.

I went into their dressing-room shortly after the end because I had swapped kit with James Small earlier in the tour and owed him shorts and socks. They were all sitting there with their heads in their hands, unable to believe that they had lost. They had been typically arrogant on the pitch, mouthing obscenities and insults which do not bear repeating. They had made the mistake of assuming they were going to win, of believing what they had read. We had performed an old-fashioned FA Cup upset, but we had to do it again. We would not have the element of surprise, but the South African media turned their guns on the Springboks and the pressure on them in Durban the following week was intense.

That was their problem. Our victory was based on the scrummaging of the front row which asserted itself after a couple of dodgy moments early on and defence in which Scott Gibbs, Lawrence Dallaglio and Tim Rodber were outstanding. After the series had been won, the South Africans complained that we were a negative side, conveniently forgetting both the manner in which they had won the World Cup and the tendency of the Springboks to kill the ball. I was not complaining because it gave me the chance to justify my place in the side, but we had the ability to score tries, as we showed in the last ten minutes in Cape Town.

We left Cape Town for Durban. The midweek match was against the powerful Free State in Bloemfontein, and although no members of the Test side were included, the players knew how important the game was because we were suddenly being taken seriously. The result was the best rugby of the tour, an exhilarating performance which ended in a resounding 52–30 victory. The pace of the game was relentless and finally buried the claim that we could not live with Super 12 sides.

I came on as a substitute just before the interval and was out of breath by the break! I had replaced Will Greenwood, who had been knocked unconscious in a tackle. We knew it was serious, but it emerged later that he could have died. Jim told us at half-time to do it for Will, who fortunately made a full recovery. His tour was over, however, and he must have been very close to a Test spot.

Geech had stayed in Durban because he had a bug which he did not want to risk passing on to the players. We flew in and out on the day and when I arrived at the hotel, Cath was waiting for me. She had decided to get our wedding rings in South Africa (we were getting married the following year) and she wanted me to see a selection in a shop near the hotel. Jim had called a team meeting immediately on our arrival, and I had to run to the shop, inspect the rings and dash back again. Jim was waiting for me with his stern eye. 'Where have ye been, laddie?' I dared not tell him the truth, so I muttered something about urgent business.

Jim had a big smile after the Free State match and it gave us a big psychological lift before the second Test. Free State were one of the strongest provinces in South Africa and we had blown them apart. Neil Back, the England flanker, was outstanding that night – as he was all tour. He was the fittest player I had ever seen. He had been criticised for being too small, but we had shown in Cape Town that size did not matter. He came in for the third Test and, to me, he was one of the players of the tour, never ceasing to amaze on the training field and in matches.

Bloemfontein set us up for the Durban Test, although we knew it was going to take even more to win. South Africa had been so confident of imposing themselves on us that they had not really bothered to pinpoint our strengths and weaknesses. I had expected to be tested with a series of kicks, but they were not bothered by a full-back playing out of position, another indication of how much they had taken for granted.

I did not have such an easy ride in Durban, Honiball testing me with a series of diagonal kicks and high balls. They had had to react to Cape Town and their introspection was a source of strength to us. Nerves had hit me again before the match and I envied Jerry Guscott, who looked as if he were just about to take his dog for a walk in the park. Ieuan's torn groin had ruled him out. I had lost a defensive crutch, with all due respect to Bentos, who replaced him. Ieuan had helped me cope with the demands of the position but now I was going to be alone.

The noise at King's Park as we ran on to the field was deafening. There seemed to be more Lions supporters than South Africans. My legs had felt weak in the changing-room but the noise had such an uplifting effect that I left my nerves behind. The Springboks started at a furious pace as if to prove that the previous week had been a bad dream. Scott Gibbs had gathered the players in the middle before the kick-off, jabbing his finger towards everyone, urging no surrender. He led by example, knocking down one player after another, no matter how large.

Despite all South Africa's pressure, we led by 6–0 after 30 minutes through two penalties from me. My first kick was virtually from the halfway line. They had missed a couple of relatively straightforward chances and I knew that if I could put it over it would raise renewed doubts in their minds. It sailed off my boot to strains of 'Bread of Heaven', but the Springboks came back before the interval after Honiball had rolled a kick to the corner.

The second half was only a minute old when we gave away a soft try. I landed another penalty but André Joubert scored their third try and we were up against it, 15–9 down. Once again our fitness came into play. Had they landed their goal-kicks they would have been out of sight, but Scott Gibbs went on a charging run and used the 20-stone prop Os du Randt, known as the Ox, as a doormat. We had men over to go for a try, but they again killed the ball. 15–12.

Seven minutes later I had another chance. They had used three goal-kickers but they had all failed and I pointed at the posts. 15–15. They knew it was slipping away from them and Woody led a charge by hacking the ball 60 yards downfield. He had given his all and his body was falling apart, but he got us into their twenty-two. The forwards and Matt drove on. I shouted for Gregor to go for a drop at goal, but he too headed for the line. There were not many of us in the back-line and the ball came back slowly.

Jerry caught it and, in what seemed to me to be slow motion, nonchalantly dropped a goal. We celebrated, but it was not over yet. The Springboks staged one last effort. They could have tried a drop goal but that would have meant they could not win the series and instead they went for broke. Honiball planted the highest of garryowens and I dropped it. I was thinking of the mark but I mistimed the catch, but Austin Healey saved me by coming quickly off his wing and gathering the ball. Scott failed to put it dead and, for a few seconds, it was mayhem until we won a drop-out.

We asked the French referee, Didier Méné, how long there was to go. 'No after this, no after this,' was all he said. Where was the interpreter when you needed him? Martin Johnson wanted me to restart normally but Scott was urging me to kick it dead, backed by Jerry. I thumped it into the stand and I could see the substitutes holding their heads in their hands in disbelief. For a moment I thought the referee was going to allow play to continue, but he played a sweet tune on his whistle: music to my ears. King's Park erupted in a sea of red and white and an orgy of unconfined joy. It was like being back at the Arms Park in the 1970s.

I hugged Scott and grabbed Jerry, who had been my room-mate. Will Carling had said after rugby union went open that the Lions were finished. He was wrong, completely wrong. I was asked to attend an after-match press conference along with Jerry and, for once, I was only too happy to answer their questions. Our room may have scored all the points, but the contribution of everyone – in the team, on the bench or sitting in the stand – had been equal. It was a moment for the whole squad, not a couple of individuals. I had never thought anything would beat the feelings of elation I had when I won my first cap and when Pontypridd won the league. I was wrong. To be in Durban that Saturday was to be in heaven.

CHAPTER SEVENTEEN

A Kick in Time

Scott Gibbs and I ran around the King's Park pitch draped in a Welsh flag, taking in the atmosphere and savouring the moment. We had been through some bad times together with Wales and we knew before the tour that it represented our best chance of being on the winning side against South Africa.

The last week was an anti-climax in comparison. With the series won, the edge was lost. I was on the bench for the final midweek match, against Northern Free State, grateful not to get on because a few of us had gone down with food poisoning, a touch of 'Suzy Fever' as the All Blacks called it after their allegedly laced tea a few days before the 1995 World Cup final in Johannesburg.

With the adrenaline rush over, injuries caught up with a number of players, giving the likes of Tony Underwood, Neil Back and Mike Catt their chance in the final Test. Allan Bateman and Tim Stimpson came on as replacements along with Eric Miller and it was a measure of the success of the tour that not one of the players on it would have been out of place in the Test side. It was a total squad effort.

The third Test was a game too far for us and, in retrospect, it was as well that we had already got the series wrapped up. Had the Springboks won in Durban, I am not sure how much more we would have had to give. Adrenaline kept us going as long as we had something to aim for, but once we had secured the spoils, mental fatigue supplemented physical tiredness. We could still have won the match and we had the incentive of securing the whitewash, but we modified our gameplan, running the ball more, perhaps in a subconscious reaction to criticism of our style of play from the South Africans. We had nothing to apologise for. Sport is about winning and we had worked out the way to beat the Springboks.

I am not sure that we received the credit we deserved. Attention was paid to the new coaching set-up the Springboks had, but a couple of weeks later they nearly defeated the All Blacks. Only one Lions team had ever won a series in South Africa, and it took New Zealand the best part of 100 years to achieve the feat. There is no such thing as a bad South Africa side. Win out there and you deserve it.

The hardest thing for me about the tour was its ending. The squad and management had been together for eight weeks on what was, for me, the journey of a lifetime. Part of me wanted it never to end. It was unlike being with Pontypridd or Wales because the separation at the end was permanent: we would never be together as a group again, apart from the occasional reunion. For the first few days when I returned home, it was as if something was missing. Rugby union may now be a professional sport, but to play for the Lions was a privilege.

When I had pulled on the Lions jersey for the first time, against Eastern Province, I had broken out into a huge smile. I had reached the summit and no one could ever take it away from me. My goal is to make the next Lions tour, in 2000 or 2001 to Australia and New Zealand. I do not agree that the Lions should play touring teams when they visit Britain and Ireland. A Lions tour should be held every four years. It is, like the Olympics, something very special.

The nature of tours will change, as we have already seen. The days of sides playing a welter of warm-up matches before a three- or four-Test rubber are long gone. New Zealand, South Africa and Australia have a history of playing Welsh clubs when they tour Britain, but when New Zealand were here at the end of 1997, they only played Llanelli. It should have been Pontypridd because we were the reigning Welsh champions, but we were the victims of another administrative cock-up and we were not amused. We deserved to face the All Blacks. I am not saying we would have done much better than the 81–3 reverse suffered by Llanelli, but it was a match we had earned. I do not know if New Zealand will ever play a Welsh club again. Tours are becoming a series of Test matches with profit the main aim. I would not be surprised if in the future the Lions play a series involving Australia, New Zealand and South Africa every four years, reducing matches against provincial teams to a minimum.

There is a danger that players will become burned out. The 1997–98 season was probably my worst in senior rugby: on a high after South Africa, I struggled for long periods. The Welsh campaign started in the middle of a heatwave that August and dragged on until the end of May, followed by a tour of Zimbabwe and South Africa. It was too much.

I missed the South Africa tour because I needed an operation to remove the plate in my arm, and it was timely. As well as fighting the demands of my body to take a rest, I had had a court case hanging over my head for more than a year after an incident in a Swansea nightclub at the beginning of 1997. It should have been heard not long after I had returned with the Lions, but it kept being put back. It was a serious charge and I wanted the case to be heard quickly. The end of the season could not come soon enough for me.

The same was also true for a number of the Lions: Bentos and Tim Stimpson had seasons they will want to forget, and few of the players used in the Test series in South Africa reached the peak of their form. Lawrence Dallaglio was an exception, but even he needed rest by the end and was unavailable for England's summer tour of Australia, New Zealand and South Africa.

While most of the Lions were on their way home, some of the English players had had to fly out from South Africa to play a Test match in Australia, something I struggled to understand. Rugby may need to chase the dollar to finance itself, but ludicrous demands are being placed on players. The increased speed of the game today and its greater physical intensity place greater and greater demands on players' bodies. I am picking up more injuries than ever before, and it is not just because I am getting older.

The season is now virtually a year long, meaning recovery time is short. England were criticised by the southern hemisphere nations for taking a depleted squad on their four-Test tour, but players are not machines. Because the seasons in the north and the south are now blurred, the International Rugby Board needs to take a hard look at the way the game at the top is structured. A ceiling should be set on the number of internationals a country may play in a year and domestic programmes need to be reviewed. The Five Nations should be given a slot on its own in the British and Irish season. Cardiff and Pontypridd, two clubs with a heavy representation in the Welsh squad, kicked lumps out of each other in between two championship matches, which is no way to prepare. A window needs to be found in the season when only championship matches are played, allowing players to concentrate solely on international rugby for a fixed period of time.

At the moment, we are pulled back and forth between club and country, and that is no longer good enough in the professional era. If you are to maximise your resources you need to manage time properly, and that is not being done at the moment. Too much is being crammed in, and extending seasons is a recipe for disaster, a legacy posterity could well do without.

The Lions showed what British and Irish rugby is really worth. It was a proper mix of intensity and relaxation, players challenged rather than pushed. Training sessions were concentrated and detailed, but everyone knew what they had to be about. There was little chance for sightseeing, but we were not in South Africa for a holiday. It was important to give our legs a rest, and instead of tramping the streets, I tended to put my feet up in the hotel. I have always valued my afternoon naps, and time away from the training field was spent sleeping, lazing around the swimming pool or thrashing Rob Howley at snooker.

The snooker table, table-tennis table and dartboard were in constant use and it was revealing to watch players taking part. Lawrence Dallaglio was never anything other than totally competitive. He would not see the funny side at losing a game of snap. Austin Healey was another who played to win all the time, except he was not as good as Lawrence. 'Next time' was Austin's favourite phrase, but in his case tomorrow never came.

I had read in the past that Lions tours were made by the Scottish and the Irish, with the Welsh homesick and the English aloof. Preconceptions did not last an instant, however, and the English players were all terrific company. There was nothing arrogant about any of them. Matt Dawson and I talk all the time now, and I also got on very well with the likes of Tony Underwood, Simon Shaw, Mark Regan, Neil Back and Jeremy Guscott. Baggage man Stan Bagshaw became a big friend too.

The Irish are always the life and soul of any party, and Keith

Wood was one of the stars of the tour, a non-stop player who just had to be the judge in the players' court. Woody personified the essential characteristic of the tour, knowing when to be serious and when to relax. His effort on the field never wavered, as he showed when creating the winning position for us in Durban, but he also has a capacity to make people laugh. He was adept at judging the mood of players, never pushing too far. The Irish have always had a therapy value as tourists, but none of them in South Africa was making up the numbers and, but for Eric Miller's illness in Cape Town, they would have made up half the pack in the first Test.

The biggest influence in the party for me was Dave Alred, the kicking coach. I am surprised at the number of people who think that because of the number of points I have scored, I have little to do in training other than fine-tune. My attitude is that you never stop learning, and there was never any way I was going to regard Dave's presence as an intrusion.

The kickers would spend a couple of hours most afternoons going through routines, and anyone who had questioned Dave's worth beforehand had their suspicions quickly scotched by the progress made by all the kickers in the squad, especially Stimmo, who finished the tour as the leading points-scorer. Dave enhanced our competitive instincts: if he landed a good goal-kick, he would tell us to follow that, and so we would compete with him as well as with each other. He emphasised the value of concentration, especially on kicks which we would expect to put over. He had a routine where we would take 33 kicks at goal: ten in front of the post, ten to the left, ten to the right and three from distance. I once landed 31 in Pretoria, hitting the post with the other two efforts. I think it surprised him, especially as I had never used a tee before going to South Africa, preferring sand.

Dave's work was about far more than goal-kicking, though. He helped me improve my line-kicking, again stressing the value of concentration, and we put in a lot of work on restarts, which paid a huge return against Natal when we won virtually every one. It was a feature of the game in Wales which had long been in decline, but Dave emphasised the importance of restarts in the modern game where more points are being scored than ever before.

I returned home a better all-round kicker. My goal-kicking style had developed with the help of my uncles. I have been accused of modelling it on Grant Fox, the New Zealander who is probably the best kicker of all time, and I admit to having watched several videos of him in my formative years, but my technique is all my own. It was only when I watched myself on television that I realised my hanging arm waggled.

I have always been meticulous in the time between placing the ball and taking the kick. Going for goal is probably the loneliest task on a rugby field and you have to get your preparations right. Any interruption to your routine clouds concentration and you start to be filled with doubts. Noise has never been a problem for me – I just imagine I am back on Cae Fardre – and I have been fortunate in that I have not had many wretched days when nothing goes right.

Goal-kicking is very much a state of mind. The greatest kickers in the game, such as Lynagh, Fox and Don Clarke, earned their reputation for landing kicks when they mattered, but they were also consistent, and Dave's input proved the value not only of coaching specialisation but also of concentration, of developing a routine and sticking to it. The value of a try may have increased twice in the last 26 years, but no team can afford to go into a match without a top-line goal-kicker, as South Africa found out to their cost against the Lions.

I finished the series with 41 points, which broke Gavin Hastings's record. It gave me personal satisfaction, but it would have counted for nothing had we not won the series. All individual efforts were put in a team context. I got my chances because of the efforts of others, but to be kicking winning goals for the Lions was more than I had ever dared dream of.

Looking back, it is a pity we did not win the third Test as well. We had fought back to 16–23 going to the last quarter and we created a half-chance which would have levelled the scores. I am sure that South Africa would have buckled then, heads dropping at the prospect of another final-quarter fightback from us, but the ball was knocked on. They recovered and took the match 35–16.

The sponsors threw a party for the squad on our final day in South Africa and we threw ourselves into it. It had been a long journey, one which I will never forget. No matter what anyone says about me in the future, I will always be able to point to the record books, find the summer of 1997, and remind them that I had been part of something precious.

Not that you can live on reputation, as I was to find the following season when the roars in South Africa turned into a chorus of disapproval as Wales slumped to new lows. It was hard, I suspect, for the Celtic players to go back to their international sides knowing that success was going to be as difficult as ever to achieve. The Welsh, Scottish and Irish players had all proved themselves with the Lions, but it was only England who had a realistic chance of beating New Zealand, South Africa and Australia that autumn. Given that, it would make sense to the Celtic nations for the Lions to play more often, but to me that would destroy something which is unique in modern rugby. The Lions lamp should only be rubbed once every four years.

CHAPTER EIGHTEEN

Olé, Olé

If life with the Lions was something else, a glorious one-off, Pontypridd was a constant for the first 10 years of my senior career and I count myself fortunate to have been part of the club during some of the most successful years in its proud history, success achieved against all the odds.

I, and other players, had had offers to leave for more fashionable clubs but we stayed, not least because Pontypridd held you so close that going voluntarily was not really an option. When rugby went open, the club was expected to struggle because it was not regarded as one of the traditionally strong Welsh sides and we did not appear to have the financial muscle to compete with the big boys. One league and one cup triumph later, we had nine players in the Welsh squad and a production line which was the envy of every other premier division Welsh club. All good things come to an end, and by the end of the 1998–99 season I made the difficult decision to ask Pontypridd for a transfer. It was a moment I never thought would happen and as the words came out of my mouth, it was like a bad dream. But times change and life's wheel keeps going round. The club was at a crossroads and I turned right to Cardiff. Ponty had to build almost from new, off the field as well as on it. I could no longer be a part of the furniture.

I am sometimes envious of the players of yesteryear whose reward at the end of the season was to be taken away on a tour by the club. The venue did not matter, be it Weston-super-Mare, Bognor Regis or a more exotic location: it was bonding time. I have only been away with Pontypridd twice, apart from matches in the

Heineken Cup, and both occasions were little more than flying visits. The first was in 1992, the summer when I should have been playing in South Africa but was instead nursing a ban. The scene was the Strasbourg Sevens and I went along as a supporter because I was not allowed to play. Instead of bunking down in the palatial hotel enjoyed by the players, I ended up with the other hangers-on in some basic accommodation: bed, mattress, ceiling and, for a few quid extra, a light. We had a reasonable team in the tournament, but it was a weekend for drinking more than playing rugby and my most vivid memory of the weekend is a food fight and a restaurant bill which our physiotherapist Dai Thomas had to pay.

Dai is not known for the speed with which his hand dips into his pocket, but he was caught when Darryl Hughes, then a wing at Ponty, and I joined him, Eddie Jones, the Ponty manager, and Sam Simon, the club's president, for a meal. It was not your average fare, more a sumptuous feast, and Darryl and I were wondering whether we had enough money to pay our share. Eddie must have sensed our concern and he gave us a wink. 'It's all right, boys,' he said, nodding at Dai. 'This is on the three of us.' Dai did a double take and started to splutter. Eddie insisted and Sam backed him up. Dai looked at me with eyes narrowed as he counted out his francs, and to this day he is still looking for a way of getting his own back.

If Strasbourg was, for me, a weekend of doing nothing except recovering from an excess of beer, my next tour with the club was a little different. We played Northern Transvaal in March 1995 on a Wednesday night in between league and cup matches. It meant flying out and back in four days, but it was worth it to play one of the top provincial sides in the world on a Test ground, Loftus Versfeld. I had never been to South Africa, but I was to fly out there two more times that year with Wales.

The Northern Transvaal team was packed with internationals and Dennis John was taking the match seriously. When the province's sponsors thoughtfully packed a case of beer on our team coach, Dennis erupted and ordered that it be removed. Mineral water and sodas had to do us until the match was over, which did not prove much to the liking of the non-playing entourage!

The South African team beat us 31–12, but not before we had given them something to think about. There was nothing in it going into the final quarter and there had been a number of outbreaks of fighting. It was no friendly, and their scrum half, the Springbok Joost van der Westhuizen, caught Nigel Bezani, our rugged prop, with a belting punch which split open Baz's lip. He went off for running repairs, and the way the doctor told it afterwards had us in fits. He had taken one look at Baz's lips and wondered how he could prevent them falling apart. He eventually stitched everything back together but told Baz that there was no way he could go back on, that he had taken too heavy a knock and that he risked permanent damage if he took another blow. 'Rubbish,' said Baz, easing himself off the couch. 'There's nothing wrong with me. Watch.' He headed for an open door, missed it by a couple of yards and crashed head first into the wall. The doctor had his way, and so did we because Northerns consented to swap jerseys with us after the match, something they did not usually do.

I believe the game was the biggest single factor in our emergence the following year from nearly men to winners. We learned a lot, and although we lost to Swansea in the 1995 cup final, we returned to lift the trophy the following year and in 1997 lost only two matches to become the champions of Wales. Not bad for a valley club.

There are similarities between Pontypridd and Wimbledon Football Club. The gang was pretty crazy when I joined Ponty, characters running through the side. Newcomers would take a lot of stick and we were not to everyone's taste. In the first season of leagues, we were about to leave on the bus for Neath, who were then the best side in Wales. Spike Watkins asked to inspect the kit and exploded. 'We are not wearing red jerseys,' he said. 'Neath are the home team and it is up to them to change.' Someone suggested to Spike – fairly timidly, because he was not the sort of man you would volunteer to have an argument with – that as Neath did not have a change strip, would it not be a good idea to just get down there and get on with it.

No, said Spike, it was not only not a good idea, it was also a non-starter. Unless the kit was changed, he said, the bus was not leaving. We sat there as the row raged, but once it was clear that Spike was not going to change his mind, the red kit was replaced by black and we braced ourselves for the explosion of Neath – because their manager, Brian Thomas, was as uncompromising as Spike. Indeed, Thomas went ballistic and complained to the media afterwards that we were 'noisy upstarts' trying to be a poor man's Neath. Thomas, a former Neath and Wales second row, had helped turn the club around from under-achievers to one of the strongest in Britain and he was effectively paying us a compliment. We were a similar club to Neath: unfashionable and not particularly loved outside our boundaries. Neath had forged an identity and we were trying to do the same.

Spike's ruse very nearly worked. We only lost the match by a point and that was due to a try which should never have been awarded. Neath were a real force then, and perhaps it was fitting that our first major trophy should have been achieved at their expense in the 1996 Swalec Cup final.

I remember complaining to Sam Simon the day we were playing Swansea in a cup match at Sardis Road that we rarely defeated a big side. 'When is it going to happen?' I asked Sam. 'One day soon,' was his reply. After we had won 13–3, he burst into the dressing-room and said, 'I told you so. I just did not expect it so soon.'

The link between the Pontypridd committee and the players is closer than at most clubs. Things are run pretty much for the players and I had few complaints about the way the club treated me. Eddie Jones, the manager whose resignation in the summer of 1999 was a big blow to the club, ensured the interests of the club were looked after properly. The policy had been to ensure that before players joined us, they were looked at to see if they would blend in. In my last year at Sardis Road that changed and we started to lose our identity. It used to be far more than a question of seeing who was available, but we ended up making some wrong signings.

The ethos of the club has been perpetuated by players retaining links when they retire. Eddie is a former Pontypridd captain and coach and Sam played for and coached the club, and that continuity is essential for an outfit like Pontypridd. It is different from Cardiff, who are more cosmopolitan in their outlook and who know that, however many indifferent seasons they have, there will always be a magnetism about their name. There is a romance to them not associated with clubs such as Pontypridd, Neath, Aberavon and Ebbw Vale which were largely forged through local industries.

The fortunes of valley clubs, even in the days of amateurism, reflected the economic circumstances of the time and many came close to folding in the inter-war years, a period when Cardiff ran two first teams for a time. It is what has always made Cardiff the team to beat, and so when the 1997–98 season was marred by the uncertainty over their future – were they going to be playing in England or in Wales? – the future of the whole Welsh club game was at stake.

The response of the WRU was to corral all its member clubs into a hall for an emergency general meeting, wave a big stick at them and get them to agree that Cardiff should be expelled unless they signed themselves to a binding agreement with the Union for ten years. Not only was the issue not properly addressed, but Cardiff were being shown the door despite the ramifications that would have on the Welsh game.

Cardiff were my team as a youngster but I am glad I made my name at Pontypridd. It means a considerable amount more to have proved myself at an unfashionable side rather than world-famous Cardiff. I did not take the easy road. Perhaps I would not have achieved as much had I started my career at Cardiff where the burden of expectation is always high. When I went there in the summer of 1999, I had little left to prove.

The crowning moment with Pontypridd was winning the league in 1997, my first year as captain. We sealed the title at Bridgend but the WRU did not have a trophy to present us with – which was probably just as well, because my arm injury meant I had to watch the match from the stand and waving metal around would not have done me much good.

We did not need a trophy that day. It seemed as if the whole of Pontypridd was at the Brewery Field, chants of 'Olé, Olé' booming out so loudly throughout the evening that they would surely have been heard back at Sardis Road. It was a moment I will always cherish, because for players like Phil John, Baz and Steele Lewis, guys in their thirties who had been at the club for many years and who could have been forgiven for contemplating retirement, it was a crowning achievement. I rate Phil and Stella as two of the best players of their generation who were never capped by Wales, and they always gave their all for the club.

They set high standards and were not slow to round on someone who, they felt, had not pulled his weight in a match. You knew immediately when you met them just how much Pontypridd meant to them. They could both have moved elsewhere and were linked with other clubs, but Ponty's pull is strong, more emotional than financial, and at the moment of reckoning they could not bring themselves to turn their backs on something which meant so much to them.

I often made the headlines because of the points I scored, but we were not a one-man band. They say a team is only as strong as its weakest link, and there was no one in the side who was not worth his place. The Lions reminded me so much of Ponty: it was a squad effort with everyone rooting for each other, in the side or not. Dennis John set high standards and the players all responded.

The seeds for our championship success had been sown in the previous few years. After Dennis's arrival, our seasons were characterised by bursts of successive victories punctuated by unexpected defeats. We thought we had arrived in 1995 when we faced Swansea in the Swalec Cup final, but it was a day when my kicking touch deserted me and we lost 17–12. It was a chastening experience: we had let down the supporters and it could have been the last chance for a number of players. We resolved there and then that we would be back, and we were the following year when we met Neath.

There was pressure on us. We had been labelled bridesmaids whose big day would never come and it was definitely the last chance for some. Baz was retiring at the end of the season having reached the age of 39 (that was what he admitted to but you never can tell with props!). We all wanted him to go bearing the Swalec Cup but Neath were enjoying a renaissance, having come from nowhere to head the first division. They were chasing the double in a title race with Cardiff which was going down to the wire, and Neath's final league match was against us at the Gnoll.

We did not mind them having the league, but the cup had never been won by Pontypridd and it was coming home. We had won at Newbridge in an earlier round and that was a good omen for us because it was a ground where we had often struggled. We were confident, but before we knew it we were 22–9 down against a side playing with total assurance. In years past our heads would have dropped, but most of their chances had been the result of our mistakes and we kept our heads. Baz played the game of his life, leading from the front. The previous week he had taken a shocking punch in a league match against our local rivals, Treorchy, and it was touch and go for a while whether he would play in the final. Two broken legs would not have denied Baz his day, though. Paul John had an outstanding game at scrum half and we stormed back to win 29–22, Neath left to rue the lack of a recognised goal-kicker. It was, by common consent, one of the most thrilling finals ever staged and it was a record points aggregate, but all that mattered to us was that we had something to show our superb supporters.

The National Stadium became a sea of red, white and black and it was ironic that, in the first season of rugby as a professional sport, a domestic honour went to a club which placed great store on traditional values. Our attention turned immediately to the league, not because we had a couple of matches left to play, against the title contenders Cardiff and Neath, but because that was our goal the following year.

Neath went on to take the title. We had held Cardiff to a draw, although we were denied only by one of the most remarkable tries I have ever seen. Nigel Walker took the ball on his own line and the Flash was away. By the time he touched down under our posts, Sardis Road was like a battlefield, with bodies strewn everywhere. He always seems to pull out something special against us. He scored one try from a scrum, cutting in between Stella and me. There was not much room, but neither of us laid a hand on him and just stood looking at each other. I had always thought that Billy Whizz was the stuff of comics. I would love to have his pace for a day.

I was elected the captain in succession to Baz that summer and sat down with Dennis to plan the way ahead. Our priority was to target games that we had a habit of losing, such as the likes of Newbridge, Dunvant and Treorchy away. We had no problems raising ourselves against the likes of Swansea, Llanelli and Cardiff, but our title campaigns had been undermined by stupid defeats.

We were determined to put that right, and after we had started the season with a home victory over Cardiff, who had an excellent record at Sardis Road, we thrashed Newport away but then struggled to impose ourselves at home to first-division newcomers Caerphilly. The inevitable defeat at Swansea followed, but our moment of reckoning was to come at Dunvant four days later.

I missed the match but we won 25–10 and it was at that moment that we knew the title was ours to win, even though we were at that stage sixth in the table. We put together an eight-match winning run which included comprehensive victories at Treorchy and Newbridge. We slumped at Llanelli at the end of March, but won our last seven matches resoundingly: 29–3, 57–8, 47–7, 72–10, 52–24, 54–20 and 48–15.

I did not play in any of them because of my broken arm, but at least my last club match that season, at home to Dunvant, saw us go top of the division for the first time. It was a total squad effort and we played some thrilling rugby. It meant as much to me as all my Wales caps and scoring records. It felt as if I had climbed Everest, but with South Africa looming, there were more peaks to scale.

CHAPTER NINETEEN

Brive Encounters

The most significant innovation in club rugby since I started playing for Pontypridd is, without any doubt, the European Cup, which brings together the best sides in the four home unions, France and Italy. The target for any leading Welsh club at the start of the season is to finish in the top four of the premier division, because that is your passport to Europe.

Pontypridd have played in the first four seasons of the European Cup, but fortune has rarely smiled on us. We lost to a late kick against Leinster in the tournament's first year, denying us a semi-final place. I missed the match in Dublin, having broken my collar-bone, and we were determined to do better the following season.

We did, winning three of our four group matches, but still we failed to qualify for the knockout stages, even though clubs with an inferior record to ours made it through. We won our first three games, against Treviso, Edinburgh and Bath, but we needed a result at Dax to get into the last eight. It was regarded as a long shot, but Pontypridd is not a club to be fazed by anything.

We went there confident of getting a result and we would have but for weak refereeing in the final quarter. France is a country where the home side is expected to win and where away teams are regarded as fodder. If that is how they want to play their club rugby, fine, but Ponty bow down before no one. We play to win, and Dax were made fully aware of that fact from the outset.

Matches between Welsh and French clubs in the days of amateurism had been sporadic, but most of them produced a few tales: fights, abandonments, wars of words and punishments handed out by unions. Rugby is a passion in both countries and the club scene in each has traditionally been strong. When Welsh and French clubs meet, it is a case of like forces repelling.

The greatest chance of a sending-off in both the European Cup and the European Conference is in a match involving clubs from Wales and France. The French league is noted for the tendency of home teams to win. As the former New Zealand number eight Murray Mexted said in his autobiography, reflecting on his time with Agen, 'Playing at home you go down on the ball and everything is okay. Playing away you never go down on the ball unless you have it in you to die for your club. In other words, in home matches you kick the hell out of them and in away matches they kick the hell out of you. The average French club is not expected to win away. If you do it is a fantastic achievement – and the bonus is too big to be stuffed in your boot. French referees apply great favouritism to the home side for a number of reasons: the home side expects to win at home, the away side expects to lose and the home crowd is so aggressively partisan that it is in the interests of self-preservation that the referee steers his favours towards the home team.'

It is worth quoting Mexted at length because his words came true for Pontypridd in Dax and then in Brive. At the moment both matches were tilting our way, refereeing decisions started to go against us. The crowds are intimidating in France. They are not there to watch a good game of rugby but to see their team win, and so vocal is their support, so intimidating is the noise they make, that they are like a 16th player.

We were determined to put that to our advantage in Dax. The noise and the threats did not put us off. We were boys from the Welsh valleys. We had seen it all before. And more. We were not going to take a step backwards for anyone. We were prepared to meet fire with fire, and if that meant standing up for ourselves in a way the game's law-makers did not have in mind, so be it. We were not going to start anything, but if we were invited to join in, we would accept with relish.

Neither Dax nor Brive could understand this attitude. Brive had played three Welsh sides at home the previous season and had won with a lot to spare. They had intimidated and got away with it. Having spoken to a number of the Welsh players who had been involved in those matches, I knew what to expect. Brive were not going to walk all over us.

We lost to Dax 22–18, which, in my opinion, was robbery. The referee made a number of strange decisions in the final 20 minutes which helped turn the tide their way. It is not for me to suggest why his game suddenly changed, but there is no question that it did and we found it very frustrating. Worse was to come in Brive, and it is imperative that the organisers of the European Cup ensure that top English referees take charge of matches between Welsh and French clubs. With respect to Irish and Scottish officials, they are not used to the intensity of such games. They are brought up in a totally different environment. It is no good saying that the European Cup is the premier tournament in Europe – although its future has been brought into question by the boycott of the English clubs from the start of the 1998–99 season – if controversy is to be continually thrown up because of refereeing standards. Just as the competition is about the best players taking part, it is the same with referees.

I have no hesitation in putting our defeat in Brive in September 1997 down to the referee that day, Scotland's Ed Murray. We were leading in the last minute when he awarded a try to Brive after a pile of forwards had crashed over the line, even though there was no evidence of anyone grounding the ball. It was a popular decision with the home supporters, but it was one which defied logic and belief. I have still not got over it and it was no consolation a few months later when, after a championship match, a leading international referee told me that there was no way the try should have been given.

Brive sneaked it 32–31, but it was an injustice. There was a sense before the game of what was going to happen. There was an intensity about the build-up and our manager, Eddie Jones, talked about the need to show the old Pontypridd fire because it was going to be trench warfare. He was right.

Brive were the European Cup holders having beaten Leicester in the 1997 final with a breathless display of running rugby. There was no doubting their quality, but, as in all French sides, beauty was balanced by brutality. Against us, it was not enough to look to win by being enterprising. They had to show how macho they were. They may have got away with it against Cardiff in the previous season's semi-final, but they were not going to mess about with us. As we lined up in the tunnel, some of their players were indulging in a bout of verbal fisticuffs, but we resolved to maintain our discipline until provoked. But if they started something, we were prepared to finish it. They would have it their way: if they wanted to play rugby, fine; but if they wanted a scrap, they would have one.

It did not take them long to set out their stall and we quickly found that anything went. The chief protagonist was their captain, Philippe Carbonneau, one of the finest scrum halves in the world but also one of the most temperamental. He indulged in every trick going: butting, gouging and kneeing, as well as punching. How he remained on the field is an unfathomable mystery, one which only the referee and his two touch judges can solve. His excesses are all there on video and I have watched the match countless times, still struggling to work out how we lost.

The major talking point of the game should have been the final try, but nothing excites chatter in rugby like a big punch-up, which happened after 20 minutes. There was a scrum on their line and a group of Brive players pounced on our number eight, Dale McIntosh. The Chief had been having an outstanding match. A New Zealander who had become a naturalised man of the Welsh valleys, Chiefy plays his rugby going forward and does not take any prisoners. When we had beaten Bath the previous season, his tackling had been so awesome that their forwards had been queuing up not to receive the ball.

We had taken an early lead and Brive did not like it. Carbonneau was constantly bellyaching, complaining to me about Phil John, who was in their faces all the time. I told him to shut up and get on with it but it was clear that the match was going to erupt. As soon as four of them jumped Dale, pinning him down and raining punches on him, we all piled in on cue. We had said beforehand that if they set on one of us they were taking on all 15, and no one held back. The mother of all punch-ups resulted and it took a good few minutes for the officials to cool things down.

The upshot was that Dale and their flanker, Lionel Mallier, were both sent off. As he walked from the field, Dale gave a 'thumbs up' to the jeering crowd, an action for which he was threatened with an extra ban on top of the 30 days he received for punching. There was no way he should have been dismissed. Not only was he defending himself, but the entire Pontypridd side weighed in to support him. I asked the referee afterwards to recommend to the match commissioner that no action be taken against the pair because everyone had been involved, but he would not have any of it. Why do officials never admit that they may occasionally get it wrong?

We seemed to take the blame afterwards for the violence, but there is no doubt that Brive threw the first punch. They were playing at home and they wanted us to know what was expected of us. They picked on the wrong crowd. The Brive coach Laurent Seigne afterwards called us 'semi-civilised animals', which I suppose, for a man used to warming his forwards for battle by getting them to bang their heads against the dressing-room walls, was a compliment.

Seigne was merely defending his side, which is fair enough. And, after what was to happen in the town later that night, the French Rugby Federation also weighed in behind Brive. From the Welsh Rugby Union there was only the sound of silence. The Pontypridd club was not given any backing but was left to face the music on its own. Never mind that we had taken part in a cracking game of rugby, that we had only been denied a rare Welsh victory on French soil by a refereeing error and that we had been the victims rather than the aggressors; our own union ignored us.

We are used to doing things our way in Pontypridd but it was hypocritical when the organisers of the European Cup fined both Pontypridd and Brive for the brawl on the field. Other clubs, and players, had got away with far worse. We were made scapegoats, and if things were that bad, why weren't the referee and his two touch judges brought to account?

We could have cited Carbonneau for a variety of offences, and we let that be known at the disciplinary hearing held at the end of the match for the two players who had been sent off. He flew into a rage but we had no intention of calling him into account, even if his antics were way out of order and the wrong side of the threshold between intimidation and dangerous play. He was soon dropped from the French squad and told to clean up his act, returning to play a major part in France's second consecutive Grand Slam. Why he feels the need to indulge in foul play is beyond me, because he is a terrific footballer. I admire him as a player, but I will never respect him.

He'd make a pretty good actor, though. He failed to appear for the return match in Pontypridd two weeks later, claiming he had suffered serious injuries after a fight broke out in a bar haunted by the Brive players on the night of our narrow defeat. We had been invited to join them and duly turned up. In retrospect, we should have stayed away. There had been a hostile undercurrent all afternoon. Pontypridd supporters complained of being spat at and pelted with coins. Cath and her family were caught up in some nonsense when a Brive supporter sitting in the stand stood up, marched to the row in front of him, grabbed a Pontypridd flag from a Ponty supporter and snapped it in two. It was more like soccer than rugby, and when we went back there at the beginning of November I made sure Cath stayed at home.

Le Bar Toulzac was quiet when we arrived. Cath came with her family and I had a chat with a few of their players, including the centre Christophe Lamaison. It was amicable with no hint of the trouble to come. All of a sudden all hell broke loose, and the bar became like a scene in a Wild West movie with bottles and chairs flying everywhere. My first thought was to take out Cath and her family, and once I had done that I went back into the bar to find Dale.

He and I had a court case hanging over our heads in Swansea following an incident in a nightclub and we did not need any more nonsense. When allegations were later made against Dale, I knew them to be false because he had been with me outside. It emerged that the trouble had started when one of their players threw a bottle at our centre Jason Lewis and it hit him on the head. As I have said before, Ponty boys do not hold back. We did not want any trouble, but to attack one of us was to attack us all.

Carbonneau and Lamaison afterwards acted the innocent, portraying their wounded faces for the media to photograph and sympathise with. It was a sickening display of hypocrisy. If Carbonneau did have a damaged face, I would suggest it was because of the head-butting he had indulged in that afternoon. The police were quickly called and squirted pepper spray everywhere. Greg Prosser, the Ponty second row who is a policeman, and I had walked back to the bar to make sure all our players were all right and we were blinded for a couple of minutes.

The fighting had been intense but it had not lasted more than five minutes. The police were satisfied that order had been restored and departed. We went back to our hotel thinking that was the end of the matter, but some of their players made a complaint and the next day we found ourselves at the police station making statements when we should have been on our way home. Three of our players were told they were being investigated: Dale, Phil John and Andre Bernard. They were identified by their numbers, wrongly in Andre's case, which made you suspect the players were being questioned not for what had happened in the bar but for what had occurred on the pitch. I knew Dale had not done anything that evening.

The three had to stay over in France for an extra night and were not allowed back into the region when we went back to Brive for the quarter-final play-off six weeks later. The examining magistrate refused to give permission for them to come into the area even for 24 hours. The match should have been switched to another venue, but again the French backed their team and we were left high and dry, portrayed as the villains by a nation which got its retaliation in first, off the pitch as well as on it.

The other two matches passed off without incident. Brive paid a flying visit to Sardis Road and emerged with a draw in a low-key game and they won the play-off 25–20, though not before we had again given a good account of ourselves. For the third year in succession, we had failed to reach the last eight. Had Ed Murray been brave in Brive and had Irish referee David McHugh not inexplicably awarded Bath a try at Sardis Road when the ball had clearly gone dead, we would have been in the quarter-finals. Instead, Bath and Brive were to contest the final and the Welsh, in the form of Bath's Ieuan Evans, Richard Webster and Nathan Thomas, were to have the last laugh.

The saddest feature in this tale is that, in future, trips to France are going to be in-and-out affairs with little time for socialising with the opposition, another step towards the soccer syndrome. Rugby union has always been a sport in which opponents have mixed together after matches in a meeting of different cultures as well as unfamiliar faces. It is part of the game's charm, and one which professionalism should do nothing to subdue. But the stakes are higher now. What the French have to appreciate is that what they do in their own backyard is all very well, but different rules apply in a tournament like the EuropeanCup. It was a lesson France had to learn on the international field after a spate of sendings-off and ugly scenes, and they have become the best side in Europe. They will always indulge in nonsense, but they now know there is a time and a place for everything.

The English clubs ended their boycott of the European Cup after one year. Their stance was unfortunate and the European Cup had become a political football because of its success.

They do not behave like that in the southern hemisphere, where the Super 12 series has proved to be a solid platform for the international arena. That is what the four home unions, France and Italy should be looking to do with the European Cup, making it a competition which is one step above the club games in each country. It is not happening, and the whole of European rugby is the worse for it.

CHAPTER TWENTY

And the Next One, Please

It was always going to be hard to follow South Africa, but the following season was a major disappointment for me. Pontypridd lost the league title, tamely in the end, and Wales endured new lows in the Five Nations. We won two matches for the first time since 1994, but we suffered record defeats against both England and France which prompted Kevin Bowring to part company with the Welsh Rugby Union.

I had only had three coaches in my time at Pontypridd but Kevin's successor was going to be my fifth coach at national level. Ironically, Dennis John was appointed the caretaker coach for Wales's summer tour of South Africa, but I was at home resting and preparing for my marriage to Cath.

Kevin was very unfortunate. Every time things go wrong the national coach carries the can, but even a glance at the structure of the Welsh club game is enough to tell anyone that there are far more fundamental problems than who is coaching the Wales side. Kevin made a list of changes he hoped the WRU would implement following our 51–0 defeat against France at Wembley at the end of the 1998 campaign, but the Union was unable to deliver and he went.

I was sorry to see him go, even if we had had a few differences of opinion during his time in charge. My big regret that season was allowing Kevin to persuade me to play at full-back. It was one thing to fill the position for the Lions in South Africa, where you knew you had the security of playing behind a strong pack, but another thing to play there for Wales, where you were far more likely to be exposed.

I was also angry because my first two matches for Wales that season had been at outside half, against Tonga and New Zealand, and I thought I had done reasonably well. I had missed the opening international of the season, against Romania in Wrexham, after damaging my ribs playing in Ponty's first league game, at home to Cardiff. I was not too concerned about having an early rest because I had barely had time to recover from the Lions. It puzzled me that, although the WRU had created a premier division of a mere eight clubs, which meant we only had 14 league matches, the season was going to be the longest on record, and followed by the South Africa tour.

The Tonga international, in the middle of November, was my first for Wales since I had broken my arm against England the previous March. Kevin wanted me to play at full-back because my club-mate, Kevin Morgan, was injured, but I said I wanted to play at outside half or not at all. I had had a good European campaign with Pontypridd while Arwel had enjoyed mixed fortunes with Swansea. It was a big decision to make because playing for your country is a privilege and it was not with a light heart that I spoke to Kevin, but I had to be honest with myself. I was not a full-back of international class. If he preferred Arwel to me, I could live with that, but to choose both of us in the same side smacked of compromise.

Paul John was my half-back partner against Tonga in a match which was played in Swansea because of the redevelopment work taking place at the National Stadium. He had captained Wales against Canada in the summer and was keeping Robert Howley out of the side, although Howler came on for the last quarter against Tonga. We won comfortably, 46–12 – no mean feat considering they lived the match offside – but a sterner challenge lay ahead at the end of the month: the All Blacks at Wembley.

I never thought there would be anything to match running out at Cardiff Arms Park, but emerging from the Wembley tunnel was an experience to savour. We were to play three matches at the home of English soccer that season, but while there was no denying the superb atmosphere generated there, it was not Wales and I will be delighted when the new Millennium Stadium is open for business. Wales are playing England at Wembley in the 1999 championship but which will be the home team?

The All Blacks were as special as they had been in the 1995

World Cup. They had undertaken an arduous tour at the end of a long season, with internationals against Ireland, England (twice) and Wales played in successive weeks, but they emerged unbeaten. We performed reasonably well against them but still lost 42–7. We put together some long periods of continuity and were unfortunate not to score at least two more tries than the solitary one claimed by Nigel Walker: I lost the ball over the line and Leigh Davies was ankle-tapped after he had appeared free.

The pace in the first 25 minutes was lung-bursting and we did not know whether we were coming or going. The game again highlighted the inadequate breeding ground that is Welsh club rugby and why a level above it, such as the European Cup, needed to be fully developed. Jonah Lomu marked his return to the international scene after a long and debilitating illness and we managed once again to keep him out. The trouble with the All Blacks is that you are forever shoving all your fingers into the dyke to prevent leaks. Stop Lomu and Jeff Wilson and you have Christian Cullen or Frank Bunce to worry about, not to mention their loose forwards. They are a complete team, and the skills of the leading 125 players in New Zealand are enhanced by the Super 12 series against provinces from South Africa and Australia, because the competition is all about sharpening attacking instincts. It has been maligned and misunderstood in Europe for the way various laws are bent, but the whole point of it is that it is different from ordinary provincial rugby. It is a step up and perhaps it is no wonder that New Zealand, South Africa and even Australia continue to move away from the rest.

They are innovative in the south, receptive to change. We are more conservative in Europe, seeming to prefer to find reasons for not doing things differently rather than actively moving forward. The way the hemispheres approach refereeing is instructive: in the south, referees are involved in the shaping of national gameplans. They are part of the fabric. In Europe, referees are distinct from the playing side and I struggle to understand sometimes what wavelength they are tuned into.

As captain of Pontypridd, I constantly ask referees why various decisions have been made, usually against us, and there have been matches when I have been so baffled by inconsistencies that I have let fly with a few volleys. The response has occasionally been the brandishing of a yellow card to a captain for over-zealously questioning a referee's decision. I know I should not let my frustration get the better of me as captain, but having seen how the game is organised in countries like South Africa and Australia, I get very annoyed by what I see as a failure in Wales to appreciate just how the game is moving on. We are not learning and our club game is clotted with whistle when we should be encouraging movement of the ball.

The All Blacks showed us how, but what is the point of marvelling at the way they play and organise their domestic rugby if you are not prepared to digest anything from it? John Hart, the New Zealand coach, was gracious in his praise of Wales, saying that Kevin was on the right lines, but five months later the Wales coach was looking for a new job, essentially for reasons beyond his control.

The New Zealand players mixed freely with us afterwards and were gracious in victory. They were determined to beat England the following week after the English players had done a lap of honour at Old Trafford despite having lost to the All Blacks, but the match ended in a thrilling draw at Twickenham which confirmed that England were by far the strongest of the four home unions. Twickenham was to be the venue of our first championship match of the campaign.

Before that, we took on Italy in Llanelli in what was a dress rehearsal for the Six Nations championship which will start in 2000. I thought I had played reasonably well against New Zealand but I was moved back to full-back for Italy with Arwel brought back at outside half. I was angry and felt like telling Kevin that I was not going to play there. He calmed me down by saying that Arwel and I were among his leading 15 players and I ended up agreeing to the switch. It was a stupid thing to do because my heart was not in it.

My mother was angry with me for not remaining true to my instincts, and almost as soon as I made the decision I regretted it. The choice, as it was put to me, was did I want to play for Wales or not? Of course I did, above everything else, but I felt I had been moved around enough in my career. I did not have the pace for full-back, which had become a requirement of the position in the modern game. Christian Cullen had scored three tries against us from full-back for New Zealand and he epitomised the modern full-back. The way I saw it, my ability to score points was going to be needed to make up for my potential deficiencies rather than supplementing the strengths of the side, and that did not make any sense.

I went through a period when I was depressed with rugby and it was reflected in my performances. It was also around the time that I had spoken with Bath and I was more than a little confused. Italy passed smoothly enough, although we laboured to press home our forward advantage and only won by three points. Twickenham was the next stop and England's Grand Slam hopes had been dashed in Paris.

We were confident of doing well against England. We felt they were not better than us man for man and they had yet to win a match under new coach Clive Woodward. They also seemed to be caught between two styles of play: the old power game, which had served them so well in the early years of the decade, and the wider approach favoured by Woodward. We believed we had a chance if we could get in among them early on and make them chase the game.

Our tactics worked initially and we were leading 12–6 after 28 minutes, thanks to two tries from Allan Bateman. It should have been 14–6 but I missed a sitter of a conversion for reasons I have still to work out. The match turned when England were awarded a fortunate penalty. Wayne Proctor, a replacement for Nigel Walker who dislocated his shoulder in the opening minutes, was penalised for not releasing the ball even though he had been held unfairly on the ground.

England had a kick 35 yards from our posts and we expected them to go for goal. The old England would have, but Lawrence Dallaglio, perhaps mindful that our second try had come from a failed drop-goal attempt by Paul Grayson, opted to kick for touch and drive the resulting line-out. It worked, and they ended up scoring a converted try, seven points instead of three. They added three more tries before half-time. Having been six points ahead, we went in at the interval 34–12 down, having already equalled the record for the most points conceded by a Wales team at Twickenham.

We were shell-shocked, and what made it harder to understand was that England were nowhere near as good as the All Blacks had been. They were, however, focused and had been upset at some comments attributed to Welsh players before the match. Kevin had given the media open house to the players in the week of the Test and a few things had been lost in translation. Lawrence sounded off as we left the field and I tried to remonstrate with him.

We dealt with the media with more circumspection after Twickenham. We lost 60–26 and there was not much to say. Their forwards got on top in the second half and they ran us ragged. They were coming at me from all angles at full-back and I felt horribly vulnerable. My worst nightmares had come true and I went up to Kevin afterwards and told him that I had played my last game at full-back. If he did not think I was good enough to play international rugby at outside half, fair enough, but it was not fair on me or the team to play me in a position where I was so obviously uncomfortable.

I felt I should have been moved to outside half during the match. Arwel had hardly been able to train because of an injured knee and he was clearly not 100 per cent fit, but Nigel's early injury reduced Kevin's options. It was a quiet changing-room afterwards and when we returned home I did not go out for three days. I could imagine what was being written and said about me and I did not have a defence other than I was not a full-back. I knew I had had a bad game, probably the worst of my career, and after a while I had a peek at the newspapers just to get me going. I had been written off many times before and criticism had always acted as a spur.

The following week we held a debriefing session in which Kevin asked every player to volunteer their opinions of Twickenham. David Young remarked that it was not only the players who had felt the heat of the public criticism but also their families, his kids being teased mercilessly at school. It showed how much rugby still meant to people in Wales and made the margin of our defeat all the more poignant. We were determined to put it right against Scotland at Wembley.

I was returned to the outside-half position, my third switch in six internationals, but at least I had now made my position clear. My days at full-back were over, and my last memory of the position is the sight of my old mate Matt Dawson scampering past me on the way to the try-line. I was accused by some of not trying to chase the various England players who accelerated away from me, but that is like blaming the driver of an Escort for not putting his foot down when a Porsche shoots past.

We had to defeat Scotland; all talk of performance and style was thrown out of the window. After the humiliation of Twickenham we had to win, and Scotland were coming off the back of a heavy defeat by France. The squad was drawn together tighter after England and we virtually shut the media out. I only lasted 19 minutes of the match, retiring with a badly gashed eye after a clumsy tackle on full-back Derrick Grant. My defence, usually one of the strongest features of my game, lacked something that season, but at least I had the summer to put it right.

I was impatient to get back on but the doctor said the wound needed a bandage which would have covered the whole of my eye. I was shattered because I had been given the opportunity I so desperately wanted, to play at outside half again. Arwel came on for me and kicked us to victory in the second half after Scotland had scored two enterprising tries.

The feeling afterwards was one of relief rather than euphoria. As our second row Mike Voyle said, had we lost we would not have dared cross the Severn Bridge. The Welsh support at Wembley was amazing, far more than we deserved after England. At least we had not let them down and we went to Dublin in better heart. Our objective at the start of the campaign had been to beat Scotland and Ireland and look to pick something up against England and France. We were halfway there.

I stayed at outside half for Dublin and had one of my best games in a Welsh jersey. Ireland started strongly, as always, and they were fired up after an heroic display two weeks earlier when they had been robbed of victory in Paris by a late try which should not have been awarded because of a knock-on. They took an early 12–3 lead but Allan Bateman scored an opportunistic try and we gradually subdued them. I scored our third and final try on a ground where I had never tasted defeat. Scoring 20 of our 30 points was a fair return, and it left me six short of 600 for Wales.

We enjoyed a lively night with the Irish boys and it was good to catch up with Keith Wood, Paul Wallace and Eric Miller again. France loomed at Wembley in two weeks, but we enjoyed the moment in Dublin. Twickenham was becoming a distant memory and our recent record against France was good: we had won our last two championship matches against them in Cardiff and only lost narrowly in Paris in 1997.

In the build-up to the France match, I did not feel that the togetherness which had cemented the squad after Twickenham was still there. We had lost Scott Gibbs through injury and Allan Bateman was forced to pull out after his young daughter was taken ill. France were looking to achieve history by winning their first back-to-back Grand Slams but they had had a strange season: thrashed by South Africa that December, they had struggled against Ireland but were by far the better team on the day against England.

It was typical France: you never knew what to expect. The match was held on a Sunday to suit television, and we never got out of our blocks. They scored a try within five minutes, and although the atmosphere at the ground was electric, it was not intimidating in the way the National Stadium was. In 1996, you could see the apprehension on the faces of the French players before the kick-off; at Wembley, they looked ominously relaxed.

It was another bad day for me in what had become a depressing season. My opposite number, Thomas Castaignède, gave me the runaround in one of the most brilliant displays by an outside half that I have ever seen. He was well provided by Philippe Carbonneau, who showed that when he concentrates on rugby he is a supreme player. They thrashed us 51–0 and it could have been more. We did well in the tight, but their speed in the loose and their anticipation were too much for us. They reflected not so much the difference in the ability of the two sides but the structures which served the two national sides.

They were properly geared up and we were not, but as we travelled home the following day, I knew that the calls would be for Kevin's head. And so it proved. The reaction bordered on the hysterical, but merely blaming the coach was a nonsense. All the players had to look at themselves and we had to ask what purpose our club game was serving. It had been a stop-start season which had alienated many supporters: strange kick-off times, endless Saturdays without any action and a small premier division. Watching sport is a habit; when people get out of it, it is very hard to draw them back. Even my parents preferred to watch English matches on television or Llantwit Fadre than sample premier division action.

Kevin duly went, after presenting his blueprint to the WRU which it was unable to accept. He departed 'by mutual consent' and, to the Union's credit, it did not bow to public opinion by sacking him. There had been talk of bolstering his position with an assistant coach from the southern hemisphere and a team manager; Jonathan Davies or Ieuan Evans would have fitted the bill.

When Kevin went, the WRU decided to look to New Zealand for his successor, saying it was prepared to pay the earth for the right man, but what they also had to do was review the club game. Instead, a big stick was waved at the premier division clubs, who were told that if they did not sign binding ten-year agreements they would not be given any money. Only Cardiff could afford to hold out; the rest faced bankruptcy. It was more coercion than co-operation, and it did not augur well for the future.

My contract with Pontypridd was up that summer and the thought of joining Bath grew ever more appealing, but there was a snag: my contract with the WRU, which stipulated that I had to play my club rugby in Wales. If Bath wanted me, they would have to pay to get me out of it because it had a year to run. I finished the season like Cardiff: not knowing what I would be doing come the beginning of September.

CHAPTER TWENTY-ONE

Paying the Price

If there were times towards the end of the 1997–98 season when I was feeling sorry for myself, I was jolted out of my selfish thoughts by the image of my former Wales colleague Gwyn Jones lying in a hospital bed. Gwyn had injured his neck playing for Cardiff against Swansea in December and there were fears he would never walk again.

When I heard the news, I was numb with shock. Injury is an occupational hazard for sportsmen and women, as Gwyn, a medical student, appreciated only too well. Gwyn had been hurt as he bent over to play the ball at a ruck, as players all over Wales do thousands of times on a Saturday. He suffered concussion of his spinal cord and it was clear from the outset that he would never play rugby again.

That was the least of his concerns. His priority was to walk again and qualify to practise medicine. Gwyn was the Wales captain at the time of his injury and just two weeks previously he had led out Wales to face the All Blacks at Wembley. His injury brought home to every player just how precarious our profession is: each game could be your last.

You think it will never happen to you but you have to make provision. It is too soon to say whether the game can afford professionalism, at least at current pay levels. There are already signs in Wales that clubs have overstretched themselves: Llanelli sold their ground to the Welsh Rugby Union to help pay off a seven-figure debt and Neath went into partnership with the Union after hitting financial difficulties.

Cardiff apart, there is not a club in Wales which can afford to run a squad complete with full-time players. The WRU has contracted some of its leading players to keep them in Wales and I was one who signed a deal. It appeared better then than it does now, and in my view its conditions were too restrictive. One of the clauses said I had to play my rugby in Wales, which meant the Union could hold me to my contract when Bath approached me.

But there would have been nothing to stop me going back to Llantwit Fadre. The Union would still have had to pay me my money, at least until I had been left out of two consecutive squads. My argument was that joining a club like Bath would improve me as a rugby player, and that would be to Wales's advantage.

The Union's policy of trying to keep players in Wales was understandable, but at the same time it had to provide them with meaningful rugby. My heart has always beaten for Welsh rugby, but my head told me that it would be to my advantage to play in England. In the end it was not up to me: even though I was a free agent in the summer of 1998 under the Bosman ruling, I had the freedom only to move anywhere in Wales.

I could have retired from international rugby which would have rendered my contract with the WRU redundant, but at 26 that was not an option I wanted to consider. My long-term goal was to make the next Lions tour and, besides, there is nothing like playing for your country. I just had to sit tight and bite my lip.

I was preoccupied for much of the time with the charges of assault which had been laid against me at the beginning of 1997 following an incident in a Swansea nightclub. The case took 15 months to come to court and after three weeks all the charges against me were dropped. The sense of relief I felt was enormous, but I was also angry that I had had to waste so much time and money on something I was not guilty of. I had faced the prospect of being jailed if the jury had found me guilty and there is no way you can put something like that at the back of your mind.

Had that happened, I could have lost everything – my WRU contract, my job with Just Rentals, my deal with Adidas – and perhaps I would not have been offered a new club contract, and all for something which, had it happened on a rugby field, would have merited little attention. I am not playing down what happened in the club, but I was certainly not the instigator of anything and the

Pontypridd way is that when your mates are being set upon, you do not stand idly by.

It brought home the way professionalism has changed the game. In the old days, players would always have a good night out after a match and that is something I have always enjoyed. You work hard and then relax, but soccer players have had to learn to curb their social activities because they are potential targets for publicity seekers, and it is now the same in rugby. The fabric which made the game unique is beginning to unravel.

The International Rugby Board had no choice but to abandon amateurism. The major southern hemisphere unions and France had long found ways to get around the old laws and their players were professional in all but name, with jobs tailored to the sport. I suppose I was as well, because Just Rentals have always been model employers, giving me all the time I need to prepare for and play rugby.

It was the same when I worked for my father, but most other players in Wales were not so fortunate and the threat of a rugby circus said to be organised by the Australian media magnate Kerry Packer after the 1995 World Cup was real. The Welsh squad heard a presentation in Cardiff and there were stories that all the leading players in Australia, South Africa and New Zealand were signing up. It sounded too good to be true to me and too much was up in the air. I was glad it did not take off because it was not the way to go about things.

Even in the professional era, clubs will need backers like Just Rentals because the club game is not generating sufficient income on its own to sustain high wage levels. The pay explosion in Britain after the IRB's decision was largely due to the millionaires who bought a number of English clubs. The likes of Richmond, Saracens and Bedford, who had been dormant, quickly found success through the cheque-book, but there will be a limit to the largesse of even the most generous backer. There will come a time when they will stop putting their resources into a club which would then have to stand on its own two feet.

The problem for rugby union is that it is not like soccer where the club game brings home the bacon. The Premier League is massive and the clubs in it are financially self-sufficient, even if there is room for the likes of Blackburn Rovers and Newcastle United to force their way into it through the contributions of millionaire backers. International soccer is much smaller beer.

The opposite is true in rugby: it is the international game which most excites sponsors and television, but the rise of the owner-backed clubs has created a conflict with unions, a battle for power over who controls the purse strings. The English club game has developed enormously in the last couple of years and high-quality players have been attracted from overseas, but the combined debts of the leading clubs are astronomical. The support base is not yet there in the game to pay them off.

But at least the leading players in England are more fortunate than their counterparts in Wales. They do not have dual contracts, which means their time spent training with England is limited to when they gather the week before an international. The Welsh squad train together every Wednesday and the sessions are physical and intense. On top of the demands of club sessions, it means players are being overtrained, and it is an issue which needs to be looked at.

I would like to see the Welsh squad bonding together more away from the rugby field, whether it be through golf days or ten-pin bowling. Too much training wears you out and you need to be stimulated. I was drained when the 1997–98 season finished and for the first time in my career I was delighted to have nothing to do in the summer. I had never looked forward so much to putting my feet up.

It was also a time to reflect on what I would do after rugby. I was nowhere near the end of my career, but Gwyn's injury meant I had to think beyond the present. Pontypridd were ensuring that all the young players coming into our squad on full-time contracts enrolled on college courses to give them something to fall back on when they finished playing. My advice to any young player coming into the game is not to be seduced by the sums of money which are being bandied about.

There is a good living to be made from rugby. I am financially secure, not for life but certainly for the immediate future, but rugby has become my life. My poor school record and the failure of my father's business left me, for a year, seriously worried about a career. I was fortunate that Just Rentals made a timely inter-vention, but I was also lucky that I had had incredibly supportive parents who had encouraged my rugby career. My mother was disappointed that I did not put more effort in at school, but she never tried to push me anywhere I did not want to go. My parents have always been there for me and I owe them more than I can ever repay. The same goes for my wife, Cath, who has had to put up with a lot, especially when the going has become rough for me. She is a rugby fanatic and she makes sure my feet never leave the ground.

Without rugby, Neil Jenkins would not have been anything, but I am very concerned about the future for the players coming into the game today. Welsh rugby is contracting. Newport, one of the world's greatest clubs, were relegated at the end of the 1997–98 season, a blow not only for them but for rugby in Wales, but they were reprieved when Cardiff and Swansea opted to pull out of the premier division and play friendlies against English sides. I thought the WRU would increase the number of premier division clubs from eight to ten because it was clear there were not enough league fixtures. Nothing was done, however, because the idea of an eight-team premier division had been to ensure that Wales were a force by the 1999 World Cup. The fact it had not worked, and was not likely to, counted for nothing. Attention should have been paid to ensuring that there were ten strong clubs in the division.

The talent is still here in Wales, but it is not being harnessed properly. A problem is that decisions are often made on a whim at committee-room level without proper consultation. The players do not have a voice: we have to do as we are told. We are well paid for our silence, but there is a pressing need for a strong players' union to articulate our concerns. When issues like international tours, the future of the European Cup and the structure of seasons are raised, the views of players are never sought. Rugby union in the days of amateurism was a players' sport, but contracts have come to imply ownership. Speak out and you face being hauled up on a disrepute charge. The truth hurts – and it can also hurt players in their pockets. A strong players' union headed by a former player, just as Gordon Taylor heads the players' union in soccer, would allow players to get their views across without any contractual obligations being compromised. It was all very well English clubs pulling out of Europe, but what did their players feel? What about Wales's tour of South Africa in the summer of 1998? I think we should all look very closely at contracts before signing in the future.

My contract with the WRU involved me doing some promotional work for Reebok. When I signed it, I had a deal to wear

Adidas boots. I had to wear Reebok in Test matches but I used Adidas for Pontypridd, and there was no problem with that until I was hauled in and told I had to wear Reebok all the time. Luckily, I had no problem with my Reebok boots in terms of comfort and performance, but players are free to secure their own footwear deals in soccer and we should be allowed to do the same in rugby.

Contracts have become too restrictive – here's your money, now do as you are told – but the game remains the players'. I accept there is no way you can have a state of anarchy with players free to do as they please, but why should we have to sit idly by saying nothing when we feel mistakes are being made? Loyalty is a double-edged sword. Being dropped by your country, or your club, used to be a matter of wounded pride; now there are serious financial implications, but a number of players have lost their Union contracts after picking up injuries. A significant proportion of their income is cut off at a click of the fingers, and that cannot be right. The leading players in Wales have dual contracts, one with the Union and another with their clubs, and we have been caught in the crossfire. I would have thought it far more sensible for players to have only one contract, with their clubs, but with cast-iron guarantees written into it regarding availability for international training and matches.

Salary bands would allow clubs to reward those players who had achieved international recognition, using the money now paid out by the Union to its contracted national squad members. New Zealand have an effective system which rewards players the higher they climb up the ladder: from club rugby, which pays nothing, through to provincial level, the Super 12 series and then the All Blacks squad. Players know that the more they progress, the more they earn.

That is not the case in Wales. The southern hemisphere was fortunate that when rugby went open their unions took immediate control and the transition from amateurism passed smoothly. British rugby was beset by conflict between clubs and unions and their differences still have to be resolved. The players have been the battleground, but our concerns go far beyond who is paying our salaries. It seems that that still has to be fully appreciated.

The problem of who controls the game, and therefore the players, has to be resolved. In my view, English clubs should be made to play in the European Cup. It is the premier tournament in European club rugby and its value as a means of bridging the gap between the club game and the international game is demeaned by the absence of the leading English sides. Rugby's most valuable commodity is the international game and any action which threatens its primacy has to be strongly resisted. The English club owners have genuine concerns, but the problems they face will multiply if the well-being of the international scene is compromised. When Sky negotiated its £87.5m deal with the English union, what it wanted most was Test action, as was seen in its attempts to secure the rights for the whole of the Five Nations Championship.

There has to be a meeting of minds because rugby union in Britain cannot afford the politics which marred the 1997–98 season, when people were talking about the game for all the wrong reasons. It has taken New Zealanders to bang heads together in Wales, Scotland and Ireland and, together with England, the home unions are closing the gap on the southern hemisphere. For once, a World Cup was looming at the right time for us, but until the English clubs returned to Europe in March 1999, we were looking into the point of no return. We have to work together in Britain and Ireland if we are to compete, not look to score political points off each other all the time.

CHAPTER TWENTY-TWO

Redemption

My career with Wales had been a series of highs and lows. When I was in the depths of despair, the Pontypridd club was always a warm refuge for me. Even in the darkest moments, being involved with Pontypridd made sure I did not succumb to despair. Those involved with the club, players, supporters and officials, kept me going and I will always be grateful to them.

It was ironic that after the end of my most successful year with Wales, (seven victories out of 10 under our new coach Graham Henry, a no-nonsense New Zealander who had taken over after Wales had been thrashed 96–13 by South Africa in Pretoria, a tour I missed because of injury), I asked Pontypridd for a transfer and eventually joined Cardiff. It was a moment I never thought would happen: not leaving Pontypridd, because I had been close to joining Bath in 1998, but joining another Welsh club.

There was no one overriding factor behind the move, merely an accumulation of events. Welsh club rugby was changing and it was clear that the WRU was looking for three or four super clubs to emerge from the premier division to play on a British and European stage. Cardiff were bound to be one of them. They had spent the 1998–99 season playing a series of unsanctioned friendly matches against English clubs after pulling out of the Welsh premier division, but they eventually made their peace and started to attract a number of Welsh squad players, including Martyn Williams from Pontypridd.

We had had a disappointing season at Ponty. We finished

second in the denuded premier division, but we were a long way behind the champions Llanelli who also knocked us out of the Swalec Cup and who defeated us in the final of the Challenge Trophy. We had made the quarter-finals of the European Cup, just, but conceded 70 points to Stade Français in Paris. We had started the season with a strong first team but we lacked strength in depth and by the end of it, when injuries had taken their toll, we were struggling to compete.

We needed a major investment in the squad but instead we were losing leading players, including internationals like Martyn and Kevin Morgan who, like me, had both come up through the club's youth system. I felt we were losing our identity as a close-knit valleys' club. Some of the signings we had made smacked of desperation, as if the club had wanted to appease its supporters by bringing someone, anyone, on board, rather than targeting areas of real weakness. Some of the players brought in were not right for Pontypridd and, by the end of the season, I knew in my heart that my time there was up.

I made up my mind during Wales's tour of Argentina in the summer of 1999. It was a decision I could only make myself and I did not ask for any advice. The previous August, I had signed a five-year contract with Pontypridd and fully intended to see out my playing career there. When news of my transfer request leaked out, the media speculated about my reasons, citing personal differences and a lack of motivation at pulling on the Pontypridd jersey.

That was not the case. My final appearance for Pontypridd came against Llanelli in the quarter-final of the Swalec Cup at Sardis Road. I was given 10 minutes in the sin-bin for showing more than a captain's concern at the decisions of the referee. Had I lacked motivation, I would not have been so frustrated at a game, and our last chance of silverware, which was slipping away. I always gave my all for Ponty, and there were decisions I disagreed with, such as the failure to sign big-name players and the refusal to offer forwards' coach Lynn Howells a contract which made him free to join Cardiff when they came looking for him in the April.

It was time for me to go and I wondered if they would be better off without me, able to start afresh. When I returned from Argentina, I immediately asked to see the club's executive committee. I brought my father with me to the club, which must have told them immediately that I wanted to do more than chat about the plans for the coming season. I was nervous as I blurted out that I wanted to move, almost having to choke back the tears. It was a highly emotional moment, the end of an era.

They would have been within their rights to have turned me down flat, but Pontypridd have never been a selfish club. I think they understood my reasons and they said they would not stand in my way, provided they received an offer which matched their valuation of me. Cardiff was my preferred destination, but Gloucester showed the first interest. Even a year before, I would have seriously considered joining them because the Allied Dunbar League was so strong, but my wife, Cath, was expecting our first child and the travelling back and forth to England every day would have been too much, while moving was not an option.

Five weeks after I had asked for the move I was a Cardiff player, though not before an element of farce. Cardiff held a press conference to announce my signing thinking they had concluded a deal with Pontypridd. It turned out that some at Ponty were having second thoughts about Cardiff's offer and it was another week before I really became a Cardiff player by which time Eddie Jones had resigned as the manager of Pontypridd. He had negotiated the original deal with Cardiff only to then have his authority to shake hands with Cardiff questioned by Ponty's executive committee.

It was a sad way to end my days at Pontypridd, a reflection perhaps of what was going wrong at a club which still had to embrace the professional era properly. There was speculation that Pontypridd would do a Pontypool and slip out of the big time, but I fervently hope that is not the case. Pontypridd, like Neath, Ebbw Vale and Pontypool, is a club built on a core identity: community. They are not fashionable like Cardiff, Swansea and Llanelli, more cosmopolitan sides: there is an anti-establishment ethos to valley clubs and perhaps it started to go wrong for Ponty when, after years complaining of being ignored by Wales, we could field a team with 12 internationals in it.

When we made our name in the early years of the 1990s, I was our only international – and there were constant calls for my head. We used the failure of the national selectors to recognise us as a fertiliser and it meant we were hardly affected by international call-ups: we could concentrate on being Pontypridd. When that essence became diluted, when the indignation and outrage were replaced by a dressing-room full of caps, we were no longer running on empty bellies. The primeval hunger had gone.

It was time for Pontypridd to rediscover themselves and I could not be part of that. I had turned 28 in the month of my move to Cardiff and, being closer to the end of my career than the beginning, I wanted to be with a club that was going to challenge for the European Cup. Cardiff had a quality squad, an excellent coach in Lynn and, having resolved their differences with the WRU, they were clearly going to be in the frame if and when a British league came about. It also gave me the chance to link up with my Wales half-back partner Robert Howley, and I had reached the stage where I could not put up with uncertainty.

Pontypridd had been linked with several top players like Peter Rogers, Craig Quinnell and Shane Howarth, but they had failed to sign any. We had won the league and cup during my time there, achievements which will always be among the highlights of my career, but I did not feel we would be in a position to challenge for the European Cup that season, let alone win it. It will be a long time before I stop thinking of Ponty in first person terms: I was there 14 years, and started as a scruffy schoolboy with dreams of playing for Wales but little chance of making them come true.

Ponty helped me become an international player and I will always be in debt to them, though I would like to think I gave something back in return. I had always fancied being a one-club player, a rare species in professional sport today, but there was no point in hanging on there for old times' sake: to have stayed there because of sentiment and emotion would have been wrong. I will always look out for Pontypridd's result and perhaps, who knows, I may return there after my playing career has ended. The supporters there are probably the best in the world, diehards who follow the club through thick and thin. It is because of them that I know Ponty have the capacity to survive in a British league. The means are there but the club has to start running itself efficiently and commercially, and start taking advantage of what it has.

I signed for Cardiff just before the Wales squad went into camp to prepare for the World Cup which would bring the curtain down on a century of international rugby. We were actually given a chance of making the semi-finals, a notion which a year before would have provoked hysterical laughter. I saw the 96–13 defeat in Pretoria on television because I had had a plate out of the arm I had broken against England in 1997. I did nothing that summer except relax, fiddle about in the garden and visit my local.

I needed the rest and the time off proved therapeutic. Wales had not long returned from South Africa when the WRU announced Graham Henry was taking over as national coach. It seemed to me that the WRU, mindful of the heavy defeats we had suffered against England and France, wanted a complete change. Dennis John was put in charge for the South Africa tour, but with so many players missing, it was always going to be an uphill struggle against the world champions. It was a tour Wales should not have made and the players found themselves in the wrong place at the wrong time. They performed well in the provincial games, but the Springboks had had two warm-up games against Ireland and tore us apart.

What was revealed in Kevin Bowring's last few months in charge, as well as the South Africa tour, was that appointing a coach was not enough, that man had to be in charge of his own destiny as far as possible. Kevin was not and he ended up suffering for the failure of others. Wales needed an outsider, someone who could take an overview after nearly 20 years of decline, who did not carry any political baggage and who was mentally tough. Graham Henry was that man.

Graham's first game in charge was South Africa just five months after the record defeat. We were given no chance, which took the pressure off. He had not blown in like the tornado we had expected – much to my surprise, his first act was to arrange two trial matches. I thought he would have organised a few training camps, but in retrospect I can see that instead of relying on the advice of others as far as players went, he wanted to see for himself.

That probably worked to my advantage because my last international appearance had been the 51–0 rout at the hands of France at Wembley. I know I was being written off in some quarters, again, but a new coach meant a fresh start for everyone. I had returned to training with a spring in my step and I was not going to give up my international place without a fight. I was still hungry for success, all the more so after what had happened earlier in the year.

Graham is a no-nonsense coach. He is a straight talker who says what he thinks and does not confuse you by taking the round-about route. I was fortunate enough to be included in the side against the Springboks and the way we prepared for that match and the international against Argentina the following week, was totally different from anything I had experienced before.

Graham had brought in Steve Black, who had worked with Kevin Keegan at Newcastle United, as conditioning coach. Steve is not someone who stands around a track with a stopwatch in his hand. He relies a lot on his powers of motivation and psychology. He treats players as men and appreciates that everyone's make-up is different. He gets inside heads to find out what makes individuals tick and his philosophy is that you will not get the best out of anyone unless they enjoy what they are doing.

As Kevin appreciated his hold on the job was becoming less secure, he worked us harder in training which had the opposite effect to what he intended. It meant we were tired going into matches, whereas the build-up of Graham and Blackie ensures we are at our freshest on the day of a game: the one exception was the Five Nations' match against Ireland in February 1999 after we had lost in Scotland. Graham opted for a more punishing schedule and it backfired.

The heady days of South Africa and Argentina had evaporated by then. We should have beaten the Springboks at Wembley. The bookies made them favourites to win by 40 points and the Boks believed them. There was a lot going in our favour. Everyone was still talking about Pretoria and the much-quoted opinion of South Africa's coach Nick Mallett afterwards that Wales were probably the worst team to ever visit the country. No mention was made of the fact that that side was a virtual second string, but with the Springboks having finished a long, hard domestic season, we knew we had a chance.

A new coach invariably enjoys a honeymoon period and we found ourselves 14 points up in the first half. No Wales team had ever led South Africa by such a margin and they were the only major country we had never defeated. With three minutes to go, we held the lead and had not fallen behind but the Springboks then showed why they were regarded as the best team in the world by pulling away from us.

If someone had said before the match that we would lose by

eight points, we would probably have accepted it but the feeling at the end was one of gut-wrenching disappointment. We had had the game won only to make basic errors under pressure. We overcame a powerful Argentina scrum the following week to give Graham his first victory as an international coach, but South Africa had got away. When I returned home with the Lions in 1997, I thought I would never have the chance of beating one of the southern hemisphere's big three in a Wales jersey: they all appeared to be getting further away from us.

Graham Henry had no such inferiority complex. He was used to winning with Auckland, Auckland Blues and New Zealand A. He did not make dramatic changes tactically, though he did encourage me to stand really flat at outside half, in the faces of the opposition, and we developed a lexicon of moves in the backs. His general approach was to suffuse players with confidence and self-belief in the quest for consistency. In the past, we had followed a couple of victories with a run of defeats. Before the South Africa game, he said he wanted five victories from the seven matches we were scheduled to play that year. We managed four, but made it seven out of ten by winning the two Tests in Argentina and then defeating South Africa in the first match played at the Millennium Stadium in Cardiff.

Scotland and Ireland were the low points in Graham's first year. I think he was surprised at the intensity of the Five Nations, the fact that it was a social, as well as a rugby, tournament. Our problem at Murrayfield may have been that we thought we were better than we were: we conceded a try from the kick-off, but recovered to end the first half in control. We seemed to switch off after that and they ended up convincing winners. We had a very young front five that day and we lacked the experience to hold on to the lead: we gifted them points and you do not get away with that in Edinburgh.

Graham could not believe how many Welsh people were in Edinburgh even though they did not have tickets for the match, and his reaction to the defeat was to push us hard before Ireland. We had not beaten them at home since 1983 and hoped Wembley would mark the turning point, but they won again after building up a big lead which we just failed to make up. We did not get into the game in the first half and looked tired after an intensive build-up: we played some rugby when we were 26–6 down, but it was a massively disappointing performance and we were looking down the barrel of another whitewash with matches against France and England to come.

We went to France not having won there for 24 years and ended up winning one of the most thrilling matches I had played in. Graham's reaction to Ireland was positive. He listened to the advice of the players about training and told us not to hold France, who were looking for a record 10th consecutive championship victory, or England in awe. It was almost like returning to South Africa in November: no one expected us to do well, but Graham made changes at forward where he brought in prop Peter Rogers, who had played a lot of his rugby in South Africa, and flanker Brett Sinkinson, a New Zealander, in for their first caps. Ben Evans made his first start at prop and Garin Jenkins returned to the front row.

We knew the potential was there and that we had lost the matches against South Africa, Scotland and Ireland rather than our opponents winning them. I ran from my own 25 in the opening minute against France and that was the cue for a 40-minute extravaganza of running rugby. We had maybe kicked too much in the opening two matches, but we ran from everywhere against France and we ended up leading by a point with less than a minute to go. Thomas Castaignède, the hero of Wembley 10 months before, had a penalty to win the match for France. He missed, just, and we celebrated.

France had pulled a stroke before the match by changing the type of match ball we had been expecting. The new version was different to the one I had been practising with – like a feather – and I ended up missing a few kicks, but nothing was going to deflect us. We had had a superb training session the day before the match, mistake free, and I had a feeling before the match that we were going to do it. It was the turning point, the moment a dream becomes reality. We went to Treviso and put 60 points on Italy in another free-running display, and then came a crowning moment – England at Wembley.

The memory of our 60-point thrashing at Twickenham in 1998 was still fresh in our minds. As the match was played on a Sunday, England knew they had to draw to pip Scotland for the championship. Defeat would hand it to the Scots, but we were determined to mark our farewell to Wembley in style. It was hard in the first half: England scored an early try and at times threatened to walk away with it, but we hung on defensively and I kicked six penalties in the first half to keep us in touch.

My record against England had been poor, just one win and not many points, but it was an occasion for every Welsh man and woman to be proud. It was the last ever match in the Five Nations with Italy joining the following year and the last championship game of the century. We were seven points behind at half-time and Graham gave us a talking-to at the interval. We picked up the pace after the restart and scored a quick try. England came back, but they were not in such control and I was surprised when they chose to kick for a line-out towards the end when they had the chance to kick at goal. Jonny Wilkinson had not missed a penalty in the championship and the kick was well within his range. It would have put them out of sight.

As it was, they gave us one last chance. We had a penalty after Tim Rodber challenged Colin Charvis high and late, and I kicked it on to their 25-yard line. Chris Wyatt, who had had a superb championship, took another catch and Scott Quinnell was off on a charge. He juggled the ball and appeared to lose control: it momentarily flat-footed the English defence and Scott Gibbs came charging through. I had never seen him run as fast, legs pumping. There was only one thing on his mind and, unusually for Scott, he zig-zagged where he would normally have run straight. It made no difference and the crowd went mad as he made it to the line: so did every Welsh player – except me. I was screaming at him to run under the posts to make the conversion easier but I think he had run out of steam and he touched the ball down. He jogged past me and said: 'Just kick it'.

We were a point behind in stoppage time with my conversion standing between defeat and victory. It was not the most difficult kick I have taken in terms of distance and angle, but it was one of the most important. The crowd went quiet. I was confident because I had not missed a kick that afternoon and it went through the middle of the posts. There was still time for England to mount a final attack after Matt Dawson had craftily kicked the ball out of our scrum and got away with it. They opted for a drop goal which drifted wide and we had won. The joy was unconfined after the final whistle, but I returned home in the evening because my grandmother was in hospital having suffered a stroke. I caught up with the players on their return to Wales the following day.

That was my last match of the season because that week I went into hospital for an operation on the shoulder I had injured against Stade Français. It turned out I had suffered a partial dislocation and two bones were rubbing against each other. I had hoped to see out the season with Ponty and take part in the league play-offs, having the surgery after the tour to Argentina and the home match against South Africa, but Graham wanted me to have it done immediately and I had not been able to train properly.

My next match, seven weeks after England, was the first Test against Argentina in Buenos Aires. I had a shocking first 30 minutes, totally out of sorts. I had a kick charged down, missed two penalties and fluffed a tackle which led to a try for them. We found ourselves 23 points down and Graham delivered a rocket at the interval. He left me alone, probably feeling I had suffered enough, but we rallied and took the second half 26–3 with some superb rugby to win 36–26.

The forwards were again superb, dominating the much-vaunted Argentine scrum, and they did the same in the second Test which we won more comfortably. Winning the series there 2–0 was a massive statement and we did it playing controlled rugby, rather than the running game we had employed against France and Italy. We had won five matches in a row, unthinkable at the start of the season, and we had become a hard team to beat.

To cap it all, we then defeated South Africa for the first time. The Millennium Stadium was only a third full for its inaugural match, but the atmosphere was electric. It was superb to be back home and we produced our best rugby under Graham. We took the game to the Springboks, led at half-time, and withstood a fierce onslaught in the third quarter. The tackling was immense and we killed them off with our first real attack of the second half. The wins against France and England had been narrow, tense affairs, but we were not hanging on at the final whistle and were able to savour what was a historic moment in more ways than one.

The World Cup was looming and it was strange to think how gloomy it had appeared just a year before. Not that you can ever take anything for granted. When we were in Argentina, we heard about the drug-taking allegations levelled against England captain Lawrence Dallaglio. Knowing him well, I was angry rather than shocked because I did not believe a word of it. The man is among the most dedicated, professional players I have ever met; an inspiration. He is important to rugby, not just to England, and I was confident he would clear his name.

I approached the World Cup wondering whether it might be my last year of international rugby. Injuries and selection permitting, the record for the number of Welsh caps and for the number of points scored in international rugby were in my grasp. I had started my international career in 1991 and was coming up to 10 seasons at the top. It was not so much that it was taking its toll, but I want to finish playing Test rugby on my own terms, and not wait to be dropped. I will not make up my mind until the summer of 2000 after talking with Graham Henry.

There is the incentive of the Lions' tour to Australia in 2001 and I intend to see out my four-year contract with Cardiff, but international sides tend to work on World Cup-cycles and by the time of the 2003 tournament I will be pushing 32. I ended the first year under Graham Henry on a high and we certainly have something to build on, but I have been dropped enough times in my career not to want to go through that experience again. At this stage of my career, enjoyment is my priority and the club scene is set for revolutionary change. At least the fires of optimism are blazing in Wales again.

Graham Henry had not been in Wales long when he was dubbed the Great Redeemer. What would have happened had he remained in New Zealand is the stuff of speculation, but I would hazard a year's wages that we would not have won six games in a row, especially with France, England and South Africa – sides which had all thrashed us by record margins the previous year – among the victims. Graham did not arrive with a magic wand and he achieved success with largely the same group of players who were there before, though additions like the former New Zealand international Shane Howarth were invaluable. Graham made us believe in ourselves. As Bob Marley sang in Redemption Song, 'None but ourselves can free our minds.' We discovered the winning habit.

CHAPTER TWENTY-THREE

Dreamland

I occasionally have to pinch myself to make sure that it is not a dream and that I have played alongside and against some of the best players ever to play the game of rugby union. It was a humbling experience for a scrap merchant to find himself on the same field as the likes of Philippe Sella, David Campese, Sean Fitzpatrick, Joost van der Westhuizen, John Eales and Jeremy Guscott.

A favourite pastime in any sport is to compare players of today with those of yesteryear. It is an interesting academic exercise but it has no value. When the likes of Jonathan Davies returned from rugby league after less than a decade away, the comment 'the game is totally different now' was often made. If that is the case compared to 1990, what point is served in looking back to the 1970s, the 1950s and even the 1930s?

As a player, you are a product of your age. How much more would Ieuan Evans have achieved for Wales had he been born 15 years earlier? Would we have heard of David Campese if his career had started in 1970? How many caps would Jeremy Guscott have won had he been playing in the days when England could not go one match without making any number of changes?

Fortune has been cyclical, except in the case of the All Blacks who have been a consistent force ever since they started playing international rugby. Their barren periods would be regarded by most other countries as fertile. Wales are currently suffering their worst slump for 70 years, since a time when the Depression caused a mass migration from the valleys, with workers looking for employment in England. Rugby league exploited the poor Welsh economy then, as it did towards the end of the 1980s when virtually a whole team of internationals went north. Wales were already struggling to keep pace with the expectation which had been thrown up by the 1970s, and the introduction of the World Cup in 1987 saw the game in the southern hemisphere effectively become professional.

A problem in the past when it had come to the enforcement of the International Rugby Board's regulations, especially those governing amateurism, had been that whereas in the south they worked together in devising loopholes and ensuring that the system worked for them, the four home unions each kept a watchful eye on the others. The history of British rugby is littered with examples of unions, Scotland especially, reporting rivals to the International Rugby Board. Even after the game turned professional, England were threatened with expulsion from the Five Nations following a dispute over television money. Then came the row over the European Cup, and at the very moment that the home unions should have been working together to challenge the supremacy of the southern hemisphere, they were at each other's throats.

Rugby union may be bigger than league in world terms, but it still lacks soccer's global dimension. The traditional top eight nations – New Zealand, South Africa, Australia, Wales, England, France, Ireland and Scotland – would ideally all have a chance of winning the World Cup in 1999, while countries like Western Samoa, Argentina, Canada and Italy have emerged from the shadows. The sport is not strong enough to survive a series of self-inflicted wounds.

The upshot is a clear gap between the hemispheres, one which is based not on talent or ability but on organisation. There is a clear focus to the game in the south, a recognised chain of command and a common acceptance – even in South Africa, a country where rugby is as political as it is in Wales – that the national team comes above everything. It has to, because it is Test rugby which brings in the money.

Seasons in the south are neatly compartmentalised, or 'divided into windows', to use their expression: Super 12, Tri-Nations, incoming tours and the provincial championship. There is almost no overlap and players do not find themselves running back and forth between province and country. The organisation is effective because the unions there are in complete control, a legacy of the way they saw the game was going long before the end of amateurism.

There is a state of anarchy in the British game, summed up in the summer of 1998 when Wales wanted Allan Bateman to tour South Africa with them. 'Batman' needed an operation on his nose and his club, Richmond, wanted him to have the surgery the day Wales left for Johannesburg because the recovery period was two months. If he went on tour with Wales and then had the operation, he would miss the start of Richmond's season. Allan had a contract with Richmond and one with the WRU and he was caught in the middle of two employers. Which one had primacy over the other? Would he be in breach of his Richmond contract if he toured or with his WRU one if he stayed at home? The two sides held firm and Allan was left in the ridiculous position that two days before Wales left for Africa and he was due in hospital, he did not know for which he should pack his bags.

That sort of nonsense does not happen in the south and Allan, one of the leading players in the world, should not have been put in that position. It would not have happened to Frank Bunce or Tim Horan, and the game in Britain has to sort itself out without delay, otherwise players like Allan are going to say stuff it and stick with rugby league. The constant bad publicity the game generates in this country contrasts with the positive messages boomed out in the south. Small wonder they have won all three World Cups.

Yet in terms of raw ability, rugby in Europe has at least as much to offer as it has in South Africa, New Zealand and Australia. We are simply not making the most of what we have: united we stand, divided we fall and all that. As a player, it would be nice to think that those in charge of running the game would find some way of working it all out. Or is that just a dream?

When I considered the best players I have played alongside and against in my career, it would have been easy to have selected a full XV from the southern hemisphere, not least because of some of the hidings which have been administered to Wales. When I actually thought about it, though, I would have had just as strong a team chosen from the European nations. We just need a level playing field, but the characteristic of the south has been to anticipate change and therefore to be ready for it, while in the north we have been more suspicious of reform, looking for reasons why it should not happen rather than looking for the positives it offers.

Having chosen my dream team, I am more aware of my own mortality, but I have never taken anything for granted in my career and I have had to work for everything I have achieved. I do not have the natural talent of the players listed below, but I do have determination. If you want something badly enough, nothing should prevent you from attaining it. Sometimes pure ability is not enough.

Full-back: The position has changed a lot from the days when J.P.R. Williams ruled the world. Pace is now a required asset, as I have found out to my cost. Serge Blanco was coming to the end of his career when I started mine, but there was a compelling arrogance about his game. He knew he was brilliant and so did everyone else. He had a sense of theatre, he was an actor upon a stage, and perhaps only Blanco could have signed out of the Five Nations in the way he did against Wales in 1991, running the length of the field to score a try.

Gavin Hastings was the leading full-back in Britain for some years, although Wales had two world-class performers in Tony Clement and Mike Rayer. André Joubert of South Africa is a player of great grace, while Matt Burke and Christian Cullen are explosive runners, full-backs of the modern age.

Cullen gets my vote in the end because I only experienced Blanco at the end. It is hard to believe that Cullen will be only 23 by the time of the next World Cup: 20 tries in his first 20 internationals says it all. It was 1934 before a full-back scored a try in the Five Nations. Who do you watch more: Jonah Lomu or Cullen? It's like being asked if you would prefer a broken arm or a broken leg.

Wings: On the right, I would without any hesitation go for Ieuan Evans, a legend in Wales despite playing at a time of mediocrity. He went on three Lions tours and excelled in every one. There are other outstanding candidates for the position, such as Jeff Wilson, Joe Roff and James Small, but there is only one Ieuan Evans.

On the left, it comes down to a contest between Lomu and Campese, two of the biggest names in the history of the sport.

Lomu has my undying admiration because he coped with an unprecedented amount of media attention without losing the humility which made him so endearing – off the field, that is! He has been superb for the game because he has helped open previously closed doors and you need players like Lomu to help take rugby to a new audience.

But Campese gets the nod. Like Blanco, the pitch was a theatre to him – not that there was anything rehearsed about the way he played. He took stick in Australia for losing matches with some outrageous stunts – not least the 1989 series against the Lions – but he won many, many more. He seemed to revel in playing at the National Stadium. He made about ten final appearances there, signing off each time with a stupendous try. No wonder he kept coming back for an encore. Campo had it all, and a tongue to match. He confirmed his class as he got older: he lost his pace but he never lost his potency.

Centres: The most difficult selection of all. How do you choose between Philippe Sella, Scott Gibbs, Tim Horan, Will Carling, Scott Hastings, Franck Mesnel, Walter Little, Japie Mulder, Mark Ring, Jeremy Guscott, Frank Bunce, Jason Little and Allan Bateman?

At inside centre, there is little to separate Gibbs, Ring, Horan and Carling, but I would put Sella there because I have to have him in my side. Even in his final season with Saracens at the age of 36 he looked by far and away the best centre in England. He was deceptively strong and fast, his reactions were acute and he was the ultimate competitor. He had it all, and when I first lined up against him it was confirmation that I had arrived. I would have given anything to have been his outside half for the Barbarians.

I think Mark Ring would have gone down as one of the greatest players of all time had he not needed operations on both his knees. He was in the same mould as Blanco and Campese, a showman with a lot to show off.

Outside centre is just as difficult but I have plumped for Guscott ahead of Bateman because of the incredible angles of running he showed with the Lions. Allan missed six years of international rugby when he turned professional in 1990. Not much fuss was made when he left Neath then, but he has since shown exactly what Welsh rugby missed. He is the consummate professional and he has it all. There is so little to choose between Jerry and Allan that they would be worth a half each.

Outside half: Another difficult decision, made harder by the fact that I never played against Michael Lynagh. Thomas Castaignède gave me the runaround at Wembley in 1998 and was brilliant that day, Joel Stransky was a class act and the championship outside halves in my time have been of high quality: Rob Andrew, Craig Chalmers, Gregor Townsend, Eric Elwood, Didier Camberabero and Arwel Thomas. I was not around when Jonathan Davies was at his best and the player who returned to Wales in 1995 was not the same, but my choice would be New Zealand's Andrew Mehrtens, the best controller in the modern game. He has the advantage of playing behind an excellent pack, but he has shown his class for Canterbury and Canterbury Crusaders and he has to be on his toes to keep out Carlos Spencer and Tony Brown.

Scrum half: The current crop are all outstanding players: Joost van der Westhuizen, Robert Howley, Justin Marshall, George Gregan and Philippe Carbonneau. Robert Jones was the leading scrum half of his day, while my club-mate Paul John has been unfortunate to have had to play second fiddle to Rob Howley, because he would walk into many national sides. We have developed an almost telepathic understanding having played together so many times for Pontypridd, and his tactical appreciation of the game is underrated. England's Matt Dawson is another scrum half I hold in high esteem, but the decision in the end was between Howley and van der Westhuizen. I should have known the answer with the Lions in 1997, but Rob unfortunately missed the series because of injury and so the South African, with his deadly pace off the mark, gets the nod.

Props: I do not pretend to know much about the intricacies of front-row play, so I have gone for two ball-handling props rather than feared scrummagers. France's Christian Califano fills the loose-head berth because he does, I am reliably informed, make a nuisance of himself in the tight without detracting from his prominence in the loose. Peter Rogers had a huge first season for Wales, a real find. On the other head, there is no one to match Olo Brown, although Paul Wallace impressed me hugely with the Lions.

Hooker: The easiest decision of all. With respect to my good friends Garin Jenkins and Keith Wood, two uncompromising players I would gladly have in a team to play for my life, there is only one candidate: Sean Fitzpatrick. I thought he would go on forever. He had an incredible appetite for the game and he never eased off. It was a major surprise when he eventually retired through injury but, knowing New Zealand, he will not be lost to their game for very long. He changed the hooking position, the first in a new breed of in-your-face forwards. Look at the players who have followed him – Brian Moore, Vincent Moscato, James Dalton, Woody, Garin, Richard Cockerill and even Norm Hewitt – and you can see the impact Fitzpatrick had. Many of the characters in the game are now to be found with the number two on their backs.

Second rows: I have come up against some formidable front-jumpers, such as Robin Brooke, Olivier Merle, Mark Andrews and Martin Johnson, but I go for New Zealand's Ian Jones, even though he plays in the middle of the line-out for his country, because he is such an incredible player, grinding away in a maul one minute, popping up on the wing to score a try the next. Partnering him would be Australia's John Eales, a giant of a man but a natural athlete who for many games has been his country's goal-kicker. The pair make the perfect embodiment of art and craft in the second row, ball-users as well as ball-winners.

Flankers: I am going to be controversial, and unpatriotic, by nominating two Englishmen. I never played against Michael Jones, the All Black who, following a loss of pace after a knee operation, moved from the open side to the blind side without losing any of his effectiveness, but Josh Kronfeld is pretty useful as a breakaway, along with Ruben Kruger, Dave Wilson, Olivier Magne, Richard Hill and Gwyn Jones. Pace is a key attribute of an open-side flanker but so is awareness, and they all possessed that in abundance, together with anticipation. My choice is Leicester's Neil Back, who impressed me enormously with the Lions. To say he is fit is like saying the Prime Minister is a Labour MP. He is the fittest of the fittest. On the blind side, François Pienaar was a driving force for South Africa but I have not seen anyone better than Lawrence Dallaglio, another driving force with the Lions. He hates the word 'defeat' and always gives everything he has, which adds up to a considerable amount. A top man.

Number eight: As with the hooking position, there is one player who stands out. Abdelatif Benazzi carried France through an uncertain period, Scott Quinnell produced the most outstanding display I have seen from a Welsh forward when we played France in 1994 in Cardiff, Tim Rodber was a rock with the Lions in South Africa and Willie Ofahengaue, who shuffled between number eight and blind-side flanker, was hard to stop. Ireland's Victor Costello had a useful championship in 1998, but the number one among number eights is New Zealand's Zinzan Brooke who, like John Eales, was a player who defied convention, a forward capable of slotting over drop goals from the halfway line. He had both vision and the nerve to attempt the outrageous, as he showed against Wales in 1997 when he passed the ball behind his legs at a scrum five and set up a try. The All Blacks will miss him.

The above would make a fairly useful team, and when you think of all the names I have gone through, you appreciate fully exactly what rugby has going for it: players of enormous talent and exceptional skill. They need to be marketed properly, especially in Europe, where the European Cup is not being properly utilised. If we can have a World Cup, why not also a World Series between the leading clubs in Europe and the top provinces in the south? The world is no longer large and we should not remain within the confines of our own narrow boundaries. Rugby union has to go for it – as one.

CHAPTER TWENTY-FOUR

I'd Do It Again

A word which recurs as I look over my career so far is 'fortunate'. I may have played in an era when Wales have struggled and I may have attracted more criticism than most, but this book is intended to be a celebration. When I have landed my final goal, taken my last restart and given my final pass, I hope posterity judges me kindly. The record books will show that I scored more points than any other Welshman in international rugby and that I was part of a winning Lions team in South Africa. 'He cannot have been a bad player' is the judgement I hope is passed down.

I have been fortunate to have two supportive parents. As an only child I was spoiled rotten and my every whim was indulged, but I would like to think I have repaid some of the debt I owe to my mother and father. I do not know how many washing machines my mother got through with daily cycles of filthy kit to be washed along with my father's work clothes. My father would come with me to Cae Fardre as I grew up, passing on the benefits of his experience, but the day when the boy becomes a man can be difficult for a father to cope with.

I was in the Welsh Youth squad when my father came home from the Llantwit Fadre club one Sunday and said that I needed some tackling practice. Out we trooped, but my father had had one too many and tackling him was easy because he kept losing his footing. I gave him a big hit and he went flying. I caught him high on his chest and he landed in a heap on the floor. The next thing I knew, there was a rush of flames coming from the top pocket of his shirt. He kept his cigarettes and lighter in there and the latter had gone off. I could not help him because I was in tears of laughter as he tried to put out the fire. He never suggested tackling practice again.

I was fortunate that rugby ran through the veins of both sides of my family. My mother's brothers have been of enormous help to me, helping me fashion a style of goal-kicking which has proved so successful, and whenever the heat has been turned on me they have always been quick to offer encouragement. They, my parents and Cath have always been there for me.

You need that support no matter how successful or talented you are because there are times during the career of any player when he is afflicted by self-doubt. Criticism in the media has never worried me because I am thick-skinned, but it can subconsciously lower your self-esteem. Confidence is very hard to build up but it can be knocked down in an instant.

Constructive criticism has become a cliché, and for the sensitive it is little easier to bear than a dose of vitriol. In the days of amateurism, players could argue that they should not be pilloried for something which they did in their spare time, but professionalism means we are now fair game. I do not have a problem with that: we are well paid at the top level of the sport and we are now accountable.

The danger is that criticism turns into hysteria, and I had a sample of that at Bridgend in 1996 when a spectator got particularly personal and abusive about me. It amounted to far more than heckling and I wanted a word with him. He disappeared and was later banned by Bridgend. You expect banter, and a bit more, but it is surprising how many who are involved in the game lose their sense of perspective. Rugby remains a mere sport, not a matter of life and death.

I was fortunate to start my senior career at Pontypridd. As I look back, the greatest source of pride to me is winning the league title with Ponty in 1997. Of course, winning in South Africa with the Lions was the ultimate, but Ponty had an even higher mountain to climb. In the shadow of Cardiff and close to Newport, two of the biggest clubs in world rugby, we were expected to struggle in the professional game, but we made our mark domestically in the league and cup and, in my view, we made more of an impact in the European Cup than any other Welsh club.

We are the ones who have gone to France and not taken a step backwards. Brive may have called us all the names going, but we gained their respect and they were the European champions. We were ultimately undone by a four-letter word, luck, but we showed that Welsh rugby has no reason to be weighed down by an inferiority complex. We have been talking ourselves down for too long.

It is good to see clubs like Caerphilly and Ebbw Vale emerging in Wales because, like Pontypridd, they place considerable emphasis on their local community, whereas a club like Cardiff looks to utilise its wealth to buy success. I have always had a lot of respect for Cardiff players because the club is still the one to beat, even in an era of leagues. Cardiff's scalp is as prized as ever and their players constantly have to be on their toes.

I have been fortunate to have played for Wales, indeed, fortunate to be Welsh. The 1990s may not go down as our greatest decade, but the thrill of pulling on the red jersey is still as great as it was when I was first capped in 1991. I may now be on a contract with the WRU, but I would play for my country for nothing, as I did many times. Nothing can beat running out on to the Arms Park, the noise of the crowd reaching a crescendo and making the hairs on your neck stand on end.

The Wales supporters have been incredibly loyal, filling Wembley three times in the 1997–98 season while the National Stadium was being turned into the Millennium Stadium. By the time of the World Cup at the end of 1999, Wales will have the best ground in the rugby world. We already have the most fanatical set of supporters and rugby is our national sport. What we need now is success on the field.

That will come if the problems which are besetting the Welsh game are addressed. We need an end to politicking. Hosting the World Cup has given us a final chance. We have to take it, otherwise I dread to think of the legacy we are leaving the next generation. The rewards may now be greater than ever before, but so are the challenges.

Looking back, I have no regrets. You would always do things differently given a second chance, but there is nothing to be gained in reflecting on kicks missed, passes dropped or tries squandered. I have been very happy with the way things have gone overall. Of course there have been downs – being sent off in the 1992 Welsh

Cup semi-final, being dropped by Wales, the 1991 tour of Australia, breaking my arm and playing at full-back at Twickenham – but the highs have more than made up for them.

I have been very fortunate. I am financially secure, if not for life then at least enough for me to be able to enjoy myself for the period immediately after I retire. I have a nice house, a new car, dream employers, a wife who means everything to me, and perfect parents, and I have played for the best two clubs going, Pontypridd and Cardiff. I have travelled the world and made a number of friends. Not bad for someone who used to load skips for a living.

Cath and I are starting a family and my dream is to lead out a child of mine as a team mascot. I love kids and one night took my two young cousins out for a kickabout on a floodlit Sardis Road. The three of us were messing about, but some locals turned up to see if there was a game on. One of the things about rugby which gives me most satisfaction is signing autographs for the youngsters. I know some players regard it as a bit of a chore, but something which only takes a second of your time gives considerable pleasure to a young boy or girl, the lifeblood of our game. I hate having to turn anyone down. When we go through our warm-up routines at Pontypridd before matches, books or pieces of paper are always thrust at you as you run out. You dare not sign, otherwise you will incur the wrath of the coach Dennis John. I always tell the kids I will do it after, but the pain of their disappointment is more than I can bear. The day I know I have had it is the day when no one can be bothered to ask me for my autograph.

I am surprised at what I have achieved. I dreaded leaving the world of Pontypridd Youth for the senior game for fear that I would not be good enough. Like a young bird leaving the nest it was a case of fly or fail, and I was fortunate that my league début at Llanelli went so well. First impressions count for so much.

I have been fortunate with the coaches I have worked with, starting with Dennis at mini-rugby level, Mike Watkins, Ron Waldron, Alan Davies, Alex Evans, Kevin Bowring and Graham Henry. They are all different characters with contrasting ideas on the way the game should be played, but there is no one correct way to do anything. Variety is, as they say, the spice of life.

I still have several ambitions to fulfil. I want to overtake

Michael Lynagh as the leading points-scorer in the history of international rugby. I finished the 1999 season 89 points behind his record of 911, which meant that, on my average scoring rate in the previous year, I was on target to beat it in six matches. That would also mean breaking Ieuan Evans's appearance record for Wales, another one of my targets.

I did not do myself any favours in the 1997–98 season. Tired after the Lions tour, I had no sort of break because of the Crown Court case which was then hanging over my head but which was to take another nine months to come to trial. It was five years since I had had the summer off and it was telling. I looked anything but an international-quality player and I struggled desperately against England and France.

The test of your true character is how you respond to adversity. I have been written off more times than I care to remember, so I do not take any notice when I read or hear that I am finished. I know what I have to do to get my career back on track, and I know I still have what it takes to play for Wales. There is, though, no way that you should be judged on your past.

I hope that retirement is a long time ahead of me and I have not really thought what I will do when my rugby career is over. Coaching holds little appeal, not least because jobs in rugby have become like those of managers in soccer: you know you are going to get the chop, the only question is when.

I would, however, like to put something back into rugby, perhaps as a manager. I like the way Robert Norster worked when he was the manager of Wales, smoothing things out behind the scenes for players, anticipating problems. You have enough to deal with as a player without being distracted by hassles and red tape. A good manager allows you to get on with things, which is what Bob did so effectively.

One of the problems facing the game concerns the administration of both clubs and unions. Will Carling touched on it when he referred to the English Rugby Union as comprising '57 old farts', but the essential point he made was an inadvertent one. The average age of committees is high and it is getting higher because there is a missing generation of players. What has Will done since he retired? Joined the committee of Harlequins? Stood for the English union? No, he has continued to pursue his flourishing business career, adding television work to his portfolio.

Fair enough, but there are a number of players of Will's era, and just before, who are doing exactly the same thing. Once they stop playing, their direct involvement with rugby ceases. In the days of amateurism, committees were self-perpetuating, comprising as they did former players: you took out and you put back in. Even in an era of boards of directors and chief executives, clubs and unions still need an army of unpaid volunteers, but if players are not prepared to do something for nothing when they finish the game, why should anyone else be expected to? If Will had thought more deeply about his 'old farts' comment, he would probably have appreciated that the problem was not all one-way. There may have been too many representatives on his union, and their average age may have been too high, but where were their successors? Sitting in press boxes or populating golf courses, that's where.

I will not mind serving the game in an unpaid capacity when I have finished playing. I think of Eddie Jones, the Pontypridd manager, who spent 40 years at the club as player, captain, coach and then manager. He did it all for free, and put in more hours than anyone. Will would include him in his 57, but clubs rely on unpaid stalwarts like Eddie and the Pontypridd secretary Cenydd Thomas. It is the same with the Welsh Rugby Union, although at least David Pickering and Alan Phillips, who played for Wales in the 1980s, stood as national representatives in the 1998 election for the WRU's general committee. More former players should be encouraged to do the same, especially those who have retired in the 1990s, because the current generation is experiencing something no other group of players ever has: professionalism.

I am not talking about fivers stuffed in boots or furtive envelopes, but making a career out of rugby. It is essential that those involved in the administration of the sport have among their number, as soon as possible, players who have a direct knowledge of professionalism. A problem with the WRU is that because its electoral system is, for the most part, district-based, the bulk of its representatives are from lower-league clubs. That has to change, because, with the greatest respect, clubs in the eighth division should not have a say in the future of Cardiff. There are now two distinct games, the professional and the amateur, and there should be two distinct administrations.

It is natural that when a change as fundamental as the ending of amateurism is made there will be a number of teething problems, but the time is coming when the difficulties have to be ironed out. We have to anticipate, as they do in the southern hemisphere. The game in Europe is not just lagging behind *on* the field, but we do have something the south does not and that is population, which makes our game more of a magnet for television. That is why those on the English Union casting a covetous eye in the direction of the southern hemisphere are wrong: they should be concerned with building up rugby in Europe. Count the chimney pots.

When I was born, in 1971, Wales were arguably the best side in the world, even if they failed to beat South Africa or the All Blacks then. The successful Lions in New Zealand that year had a distinct Welsh hue, from the coach and the captain down to the key players. It is, perhaps, too much to hope that by the time the Lions next go to New Zealand, probably in 2001, Wales will be similarly strong, but we played our part in the downfall of the 1997 Springboks in South Africa, where only one Lions team had triumphed before. There had also been only one successful raid on New Zealand, in the summer I breathed my first.

I am already working hard to put myself in the frame for that tour. We showed in South Africa that British and Irish rugby is far from finished, but now is the time for players to come to the fore and make themselves heard. Sitting on the fence gets you nowhere; it is still our game and we have to fight for it.

There is no better sport than rugby union – and no better living, as far as I am concerned – and all players have a responsibility to ensure that it stays that way. I would do it all again without hesitation – well, almost. I think I would forget about playing against England at Twickenham at full-back, but you can never fully appreciate the good times unless you have descended to the depths. I have been fortunate to have had more highs than lows. Many more, in fact – and the second half has only just started.

Neil Jenkins's Career Statistics

International Record

1991

England (Cardiff)	19 Jan	L 6–25	1 pen (3 pts)	Outside half
Scotland (Edinburgh)	2 Feb	L 12–32		Outside half
Ireland (Cardiff)	16 Feb	D 21–21	1 try, 1 dg (10)	Outside half
France (Paris)	2 Mar	L 3–36		Outside half

1992

Ireland (Dublin)	18 Jan	W 16–15	3 pens (19)	Centre
France (Cardiff)	1 Feb	L 9–12	3 pens (28)	Centre
England (Twickenham)	7 Mar	L 0–24		Centre
Scotland (Cardiff)	21 Mar	W 15–12	3 pens, 1 con (39)	Outside half

1993

England (Cardiff)	6 Feb	W 10–9	1 pen, 1 con (44)	Outside half
Scotland (Edinburgh)	20 Feb	L 0–20		Outside half
Ireland (Cardiff)	6 Mar	L 14–19	3 pens (53)	Outside half
France (Paris)	20 Mar	L 10–26	1 pen, 1 con (58)	Outside half
Zimbabwe (Bulawayo)	22 May	W 35–14	2 pens, 3 cons (70)	Centre
Zimbabwe (Harare)	29 May	W 42–13	1 try, 3 pens, 2 cons (87)	Full-back
Namibia (Windhoek)	5 Jun	W 38–23	3 pens, 2 cons (100)	Outside half
Japan (Cardiff)	16 Oct	W 55–5	1 try, 5 cons (115)	Centre

Canada (Cardiff)	10 Nov	L 24–26	8 pens (139)	Centre

1994

Scotland (Cardiff)	15 Jan	W 29–6	4 pens, 1 con (153)	Outside half
Ireland (Dublin)	5 Feb	W 17–15	1 try, 4 pens (170)	Outside half
France (Cardiff)	19 Feb	W 24–15	4 pens, 1 con (184)	Outside half
England (Twickenham)	19 Mar	L 8–15	1 pen (187)	Outside half
Portugal (Lisbon)	18 May	W 102–11	11 cons (209)	Outside half
Spain (Madrid)	21 May	W 54–0	3 pens, 5 cons (228)	Outside half
Canada (Toronto)	11 Jun	W 33–15	4 pens, 3 cons (246)	Outside half
Tonga (Nuku'alofa)	22 Jun	W 18–9	6 pens (264)	Outside half
Western Samoa (Apia)	25 Jun	L 9–34	3 pens (273)	Outside half
Romania (Bucharest)	17 Sept	W 16–9	3 pens, 1 con (284)	Outside half
Italy (Cardiff)	12 Oct	W 29–19	7 pens, 1 dg (308)	Outside half
South Africa (Cardiff)	26 Nov	L 12–20	4 pens (320)	Outside half

1995

France (Paris)	21 Jan	L 9–21	3 pens (329)	Outside half
England (Cardiff)	18 Feb	L 9–23	3 pens (338)	Outside half
Scotland (Edinburgh)	4 Mar	L 13–26	2 pens, 1 con (346)	Outside half
Ireland (Cardiff)	18 Mar	L 12–16	4 pens (358)	Outside half
Japan (Bloemfontein)	27 May	W 57–10	4 pens, 5 cons (380)	Centre
New Zealand (Jo'burg)	31 May	L 9–34	2 pens, 1 dg (389)	Outside half
Ireland (Johannesburg)	4 Jun	L 23–24	2 pens, 2 cons (399)	Centre
South Africa (Jo'burg)	2 Sept	L 11–40	2 pens (405)	Outside half
Fiji (Cardiff)	11 Nov	W 19–15	1 try, 3 pens (419)	Outside half

1996

France (Cardiff)	16 Mar	W 16–15	3 pens, 1 con (430)	Outside half
Australia (Brisbane)	8 Jun	L 25–56	2 pens, 2 cons (440)	Outside half
Australia (Sydney)	22 Jun	L 3–42	1 pen (443)	Outside half
Barbarians (Cardiff)	24 Aug	W 31–10	3 cons (449)	Outside half
France (Cardiff)	25 Sept	L 33–40	4 pens, 3 cons (467)	Outside half
Italy (Rome)	5 Oct	W 31–22	4 pens, 2 cons (483)	Outside half
Australia (Cardiff)	1 Dec	L 19–28		Replacement
South Africa (Cardiff)	15 Dec	L 20–37	5 pens (498)	Full-back

1997

Scotland (Edinburgh)	18 Jan	W 34–19	1 try, 2 pens, 4 cons (517)	Full-back

Ireland (Cardiff)	1 Feb	L 25–26	2 pens, 2 cons (527)	Full-back
France (Paris)	15 Feb	L 22–27	1 pen, 2 cons (534)	Full-back
England (Cardiff)	15 Mar	L 13–34		Full-back
Tonga (Swansea)	16 Nov	W 46–12	4 pens, 2 cons (550)	Outside half
New Zealand (Wembley)	29 Nov	L 7–42	1 con (552)	Outside half

1998

Italy (Llanelli)	7 Feb	W 23–20	3 pens, 2 cons (565)	Full-back
England (Twickenham)	21 Feb	L 26–60	3 cons (571)	Full-back
Scotland (Wembley)	7 Mar	W 19–13	1 pen (574)	Outside half
Ireland (Dublin)	21 Mar	W 30–21	1 try, 3 pens, 3 cons (594)	Outside half
France (Wembley)	5 Apr	L 0–51		Outside half
South Africa (Wembley)	15 Nov	L 20–28	5 pens (609)	Outside half
Argentina (Llanelli)	22 Nov	W 43–30	5 pens, 4 cons (632)	Outside half

1999

Scotland (Edinburgh)	6 Feb	L 20–33	2 pens, 2 cons (642)	Outside half
Ireland (Wembley)	20 Feb	L 23–29	3 pens, 2 cons (655)	Outside half
France (Paris)	6 Mar	W 34–33	5 pens, 2 cons (674)	Outside half
Italy (Treviso)	20 Mar	W 60–21	1 try, 5 pens, 5 cons (704)	Outside half
England (Wembley)	11 Apr	W 32–31	6 pens, 2 cons (726)	Outside half
Argentina (Buenos Aires)	5 June	W 36–26	4 pens, 3 cons (744)	Outside half
Argentina (Buenos Aires)	12 June	W 23–16	5 pens, 1 drop (762)	Outside half
South Africa (Cardiff)	26 June	W 29–19	5 pens, 2 cons (781)	Outside half
Canada (Cardiff)	21 Aug	W 33–19	1 try, 7 pens 1 con (809)	Outside half
France (Cardiff)	28 Aug	W 34–23	9 pens, 1 con (838)	Outside half

British and Irish Lions (1997)

South Africa (Cape Town)	June 21	W 25–16	5 pens (15)	Full-back
South Africa (Durban)	June 28	W 18–15	5 pens (30)	Full-back
South Africa (Johannesburg)	July 5	L 16–35	3 pens, 1 con (41)	Full-back

Total International Record (up to the end of September 1999)

Apps	Tries	Pens	Cons	Drops	Pts	Ave
72	9	206	101	4	879	12.2

Scoring Record for Wales against Other Nations

Opponents	Games	Points	Tries	Cons	Pens	Drops
England	8	48	0	6	12	0
Scotland	8	65	1	9	14	0
Ireland	9	107	3	9	24	1
France	11	121	0	11	33	0
South Africa	5	67	0	2	21	0
Argentina	3	59	0	7	14	1
New Zealand	2	11	0	1	2	1
Australia	3	13	0	2	3	0
Zimbabwe	2	29	1	6	4	0
Namibia	1	13	0	2	3	0
Japan	2	37	1	10	4	0
Canada	3	70	1	4	19	0
Portugal	1	22	0	11	0	0
Spain	1	19	0	5	3	0
Tonga	2	34	0	2	10	0
Western Samoa	1	9	0	0	3	0
Romania	1	11	0	1	3	0
Italy	4	83	1	9	19	1
Fiji	1	14	1	0	3	0
Barbarians	1	6	0	3	0	0
Total	**67**	**781**	**8**	**98**	**178**	**4**

Top World Test Scorers (up to September 1999)

Michael Lynagh	Australia	911
Neil Jenkins	**Wales**	**879 (including 41 for British and Irish Lions)**
Gavin Hastings	Scotland	733 (including 66 for British and Irish Lions)
Diego Domínguez	Italy	687
Grant Fox	New Zealand	645

Pontypridd Record

Season	Matches	Tries	Pens	Cons	Drops	Pts	Ave
1989–90	2	1	0	0	0	4	2.0
1990–91	21	5	29	26	6	177	8.4
1991–92	28	12	53	44	1	298	10.6
1992–93	21	14	46	26	4	272	12.9
1993–94	24	9	77	36	2	354	14.7
1994–95	24	8	66	63	2	370	15.4
1995–96	25	16	65	74	2	*429	17.2
1996–97	20	7	64	70	1	370	18.5
1997–98	27	4	62	66	2	344	12.7
1998–99	21	4	59	64	0	325	15.5
Total	**213**	**80**	**521**	**469**	**20**	***2,943**	**13.8**

* denotes club record

Other Matches (non-Tests)

	Matches	Tries	Pens	Cons	Drops	Pts	Ave
Wales A/B	5	3	9	9	0	59	11.8
Wales tours	8	1	7	30	0	86	10.8
Lions	3+2	2	9	16	0	69	12.8
Wales U/21	2	1	5	3	0	25	12.5
Barbarians	1	2	0	7	0	24	24.0
Total	**19+2**	**9**	**30**	**65**	**0**	**263**	**12.5**

All First-Class Rugby (up to 30 September 1999)

Matches	Tries	Pens	Cons	Drops	Pts	Ave
304+2	98	758	635	24	4081	13.4